THE TEACH YOURSELF BOOKS
EDITED BY LEONARD CUTTS

SAILING

Uniform with this volume

and in the same

series

Teach Yourself Amateur Acting
Teach Yourself Archery
Teach Yourself Athletics
Teach Yourself Badminton
Teach Yourself Billiards and Snooker
Teach Yourself Bowls
Teach Yourself Canasta
Teach Yourself Card Games for Two
Teach Yourself Chess
Teach Yourself Conjuring
Teach Yourself Contract Bridge
Teach Yourself Cricket
Teach Yourself Cycling
Teach Yourself Fishing
Teach Yourself Fly Fishing
Teach Yourself Golf
Teach Yourself Hockey
Teach Yourself Indoor Aquaria
Teach Yourself Judo
Teach Yourself Lawn Tennis
Teach Yourself Modern (Ballroom) Dancing
Teach Yourself Motoring for Beginners
Teach Yourself Motor Boating
Teach Yourself Motor Cycling and Scootering for Beginners
Teach Yourself Mountain Climbing
Teach Yourself Rugby Football
Teach Yourself Soccer
Teach Yourself Stamp Collecting
Teach Yourself Swimming

TEACH YOURSELF
SAILING

By
C. TYRRELL LEWIS

THE ENGLISH UNIVERSITIES PRESS LTD
102 NEWGATE STREET
LONDON, E.C.I

First printed . *1947*
This impression *1962*

Made and Printed in Great Britain for the English Universities Press Ltd., London
by C. Tinling & Co., Ltd., Liverpool, London and Prescot.

CONTENTS

CHAPTER   PAGE

I. A BEGINNER'S DINGHY . . . 9

II. THE FIRST VENTURE . . . 20

III. TACKING AND RUNNING . . . 33

IV. DYNAMICS APPLIED TO SAILING . . 49

V. GUNTER LUGSAILS AND JIBS . . 64

VI. MOORINGS, AND HANDLING HEADSAILS . 75

VII. VARIOUS RIGS 91

VIII. SELECTING AND BUYING A BOAT . 106

IX. THE CARE OF HULL AND GEAR . 117

X. CRUISING PREPARATIONS . . . 127

XI. ESTUARY CRUISING 136

XII. THE OPEN COAST 149

XIII. RACING 155

XIV. EMERGENCIES AND EXPEDIENTS . . 163

INDEX 175

ILLUSTRATIONS

FIG.		PAGE
1.	The Anatomy of a Dinghy	8
2.	The Standing Lugsail	14
3.	Wooden Cleat	15
4.	Metal Jam Cleat	15
5.	Roped Stropped Block	16
6.	Internally Iron Bound Block . . .	16
7.	A Thumb Cleat	16
8.	The Tack Purchase	17
9.	Mainsheet with Whip Purchase and Horse	18
10.	The Slippery Hitch	26
11.	The Safe Way of Turning Down Wind .	37
12.	A Reef Tied Down	42
13A & B.	The Reef Knot	44
14.	A Single Bow	45
15.	Diagram, reaching	51
16.	Diagram, close hauled	51
17.	Diagram, slot effect	55
18.	Spinnaker and Mainsail	60
19.	The Gunter Lugsail	66
20A.	A Plain Goose-neck	67
20B.	A Goose-neck with revolving boom . .	68

ILLUSTRATIONS

FIG.		PAGE
21.	A Gunter Yard and its Fittings . .	71
22.	An Iron Bumkin	73
23.	A Yacht's Mooring	76
24.	A Sheet Bend	79
25.	Tubular Jam Cleat for Jib Sheets . .	83
26.	The Standing Rigging	93
27.	Bermudian Sail Attachments . . .	95
28.	A Jointed Mast	96
29.	A Dipping Lug	100
30.	A Chinese Lugsail	103
31.	A Bermudian Rigged Sharpie . .	114
32.	An Effective Bailer	130
33.	Going in, " Cans " to port and " Cones " to starboard	138
34.	Beacon Marking Sandbank . . .	139
35.	A Marshy Creek with Spar Buoy and " Perches "	140

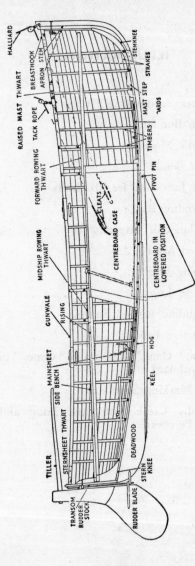

Fig. 1. The anatomy of a dinghy.

TILLER
SIDE BENCH
STERNSHEET THWART
MAINSHEET
GUNWALE
RISING
MIDSHIP ROWING THWART
FORWARD ROWING THWART
TACK ROPE
RAISED MAST THWART
BREASTHOOK
APRON STEM
HALLIARD
STEMKNEE
STRAKES
MAST STEP
ARDS
TIMBERS
PIVOT PIN
CENTREBOARD CASE
CLEATS
CENTREBOARD IN LOWERED POSITION
HOG
KEEL
DEADWOOD
STERN KNEE
RUDDER BLADE
TRANSOM
RUDDER STOCK

CHAPTER I

A BEGINNER'S DINGHY

THE acquisition of self-confidence is more than half the battle in mastering any technique, and it comes easiest where the implements are simple. Mastery follows self-confidence, and in turn makes possible the control of more complex and sensitive mechanism; but, ever to attain to genuine accomplishment, one must start by absorbing basic principles, and in the case of learning to sail, one's best mentor is that most simple and docile of boats the general purpose dinghy.

The original dinghy—or rather, "dinghee"—was a Bombay waterman's boat, a full-bodied little weight carrier, and our ordinary general purpose or yacht's tender dinghies have much the same qualities, though they are very different in rig and appearance. In shape the British dinghy suggests a giant walnut shell, a pot-bellied little boat almost half as broad as it is long. So shaped, of course it is not fast, but it is easy to handle both with oars and under sail, and—greatest of virtues from the beginner's point of view—compared with other small boats, it is notably stable.

The constructional details of a dinghy are shown in Fig. 1, while the nomenclature of her sailing gear will be found in Fig. 2. The technical names and terms connected with small-craft are confusing in the extreme, coming down to us from the beginnings of civilization and from every race under heaven. It is, none the less, essential to grasp their meanings, because there is so much about a boat and its management that is of an individual kind and without parallel ; the result being that one cannot convey one's meaning in popular language.

On the above grounds no attempt is made in this small book to avoid the use of technicalities ; but as each is introduced it is followed by a short explanation in brackets, which, together with the context will, it is hoped, convey a clear impression. No glossary is included, because it is the context that mainly explains each term, and without that it would take impracticably long explanation.

But let us " get to the 'osses "—or, rather, dinghies, which, it need hardly be said, can be divided into the good, the bad and the indifferent.

A good dinghy of the handiest size in which to learn to sail will be 12 ft. long with a " beam " (breadth) of 4 ft. 3 ins. Her bottom throughout its mid-length portion will be very nearly flat. Her " stern " (back end) will be about 3 ft. wide and so tucked up underneath that when she is carrying the weight of a man, standing in the middle of her, the " transom " (flat end board of the stern) will only just touch the water with its lower edge. The " bows " (both sides of the front end, together forming a wedge) are sharp under water, that they may divide it readily as the boat moves forward. Above water they " flare " (spread apart) to make the forward end of the boat lift over the waves and deflect the spray outwards and downwards.

In a general purpose dinghy of this size the seating arrangements consist of two " thwarts " or " rowing benches " (plank seats across the boat). The front one is the " forward " thwart, the other the " midship " thwart. From the ends of the latter there extend towards the stern two " side benches," the other ends of which join the " stern seat " which crosses the stern of the boat and has the transom for a backrest.

When rowing alone, always do so from the midship thwart, so that the boat may be " in trim " (floating level) ; but with a passenger occupying the stern seat, or two passengers, one on each side bench, it is essential to row from the forward thwart, otherwise the bows would go up and the stern down, making the boat drag heavily through the water.

It is the side benches that are particularly convenient for the " helmsman " (steerer) to use when sailing. He wants to sit on whichever side bench is clear of the sail at the time. There he has the clearest view, and by leaning back he can balance the boat, bringing her upright, when she " heels " (leans over) under the wind's pressure on her sail. If, when sailing, a passenger is carried, he must sit on the midship thwart, where his weight will not influence the boat's trim.

A dinghy's mast passes either through a hole in

the forward thwart or through a metal clamp
screwed to the latter. The foot of the mast ends in
a square tennon which, being held in a square
mortice in the "step" (block of wood below the
forward thwart) is supported and prevented from
turning axially. Under the midship thwart and
extending forward of it is the "centreboard case"
(a narrow vertical box). This is built on to the
"hog" (upper part of the keel), and contains the
galvanised steel "centreboard" (vertical fin), which
being pivoted on a bolt through the keel can be
lowered through a slot in the bottom to a depth of
about 18 ins. The "C. B." (usual abbreviation for
centreboard) is raised and lowered either by a rod
or a chain having a handle projecting from the top
of the C.B. case. A securing pin is usually chained
or tied to the case, and this is passed right through
holes in the C.B. and its case near the top, to prevent
the C.B. dropping below the keel when its use is not
required.

Some of the smaller dinghies have, in place of
a C.B., a "dagger plate," which may be of metal,
but more often is a hardwood board, and is in either
case about 30 ins. long and 14 ins. wide. This
dagger plate does not turn on a bolt like a C.B., but
is taken right out of its case, and laid in the bottom
of the boat when one is not sailing. Further on we
shall be dealing fully with the object served by a
C.B. or dagger plate, but here it may be said that
these devices serve to reduce a sailing boat's tendency
to skid sideways.

The rudder with which a dinghy is steered when under sail has a blade deep enough to project below the keel line. The rudder " stock " (thick part above the blade) has on its forward side a " pintle " (hinge pin) which engages a " gudgeon " (stout metal eye) on the transom. A similar hinge is fitted to hold the rudder blade to the keel ; but in this case the pintle is on the keel and the gudgeon on the rudder blade.

The rudder is controlled and moved from side to side by means of the " tiller " (handle) which fits into a tenon near the " rudder head " (top of the rudder stock). In larger craft a similar but much longer handle is used and called a " helm," hence the word " helmsman," which is applied to anyone steering a sailing craft, even when he does so by means of a steering wheel.

SAILS AND SPARS

Although dinghies a mere 9 ft. or 10 ft. long are to be seen rigged with two sails, and the dinghy we are considering is somewhat larger, she ought nevertheless to have one sail only, because that is as much as a beginner can cope with, and in a general purpose boat the second sail is not worth its extra complication. Her single sail will be a " standing lugsail." Fig. 2. This sail has four edges and four corners, but it is almost triangular, because its " luff " (lower front edge) and its " head " (upper front edge) nearly form one straight line.

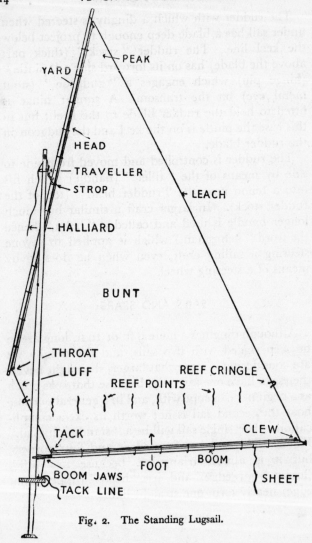

PEAK

YARD

HEAD

TRAVELLER

STROP

HALLIARD

LEACH

BUNT

THROAT

LUFF

REEF CRINGLE

REEF POINTS

TACK

CLEW

FOOT

BOOM

BOOM JAWS

TACK LINE

SHEET

Fig. 2. The Standing Lugsail.

The head of the sail is stretched along and fastened to the " yard " (spar slung at an angle to the masthead). The sail's " foot " (bottom edge) is similarly extended along the " boom " (the lower swinging spar). The yard is hoisted up the mast in the following way : At a point about 1 ft. below its top the mast has a slot right through it, furnished with a " sheave " (pulley wheel). Over this sheave and through the slot passes the " halliard " (rope to raise a sail. Origin :—haul yard). This slot should

Fig. 3.   Wooden Cleat.

pierce the mast from side to side, and not lie " fore-and-aft " (parallel to the keel), as you may find it in many cases.

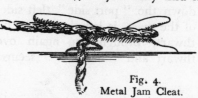

Fig. 4.
Metal Jam Cleat.

The halliard is about double the length of the mast, and that end of it which hangs down on the " starboard " side (right hand, looking forwards) of the mast is attached to the " mast traveller," which is an iron hoop of about 4 ins. diameter, encircling the mast, and having a ring and a hook forged on to one side of it. The halliard is fastened to the ring.

As a means of hanging the yard on the traveller's hook the former has round it, at about mid-length, a " strop " (ring or figure-of-eight made of rope),

Fig. 5.
Rope Stropped Block.

Fig. 6.
Internally Iron Bound Block.

and this strop is kept from slipping up the yard by a " thumb cleat " (wooden horn screwed to the yard). The other end of the halliard, hanging down the " port side " (left side, looking forwards) of the mast, is led through a hole in the forward thwart, brought up again over the edge of the thwart and " belayed " (secured by winding in figure - of - eights) to a "cleat" (securing device of wood or metal usually having two horns) or else it is belayed to a "belaying pin " (round peg

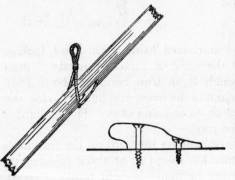

Fig. 7. A Thumb Cleat

driven through the thwart), located, in this instance, towards the port side of the boat.

In the case of a lugsail there is only the one halliard to suspend the yard and the sail from the masthead. The boom, and with it the foot of the sail, is held down close to the mast above the forward thwart by a " tack rope," one end of which is fastened to the

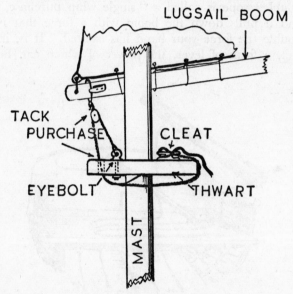

LUGSAIL BOOM

TACK PURCHASE

CLEAT

EYEBOLT

THWART

MAST

Fig. 8. The Tack Purchase.

boom near its forward end, while the other end passes through a hole in the thwart on the starboard side of the mast and is belayed to a cleat or belaying pin similarly to the halliard, but on the starboard

side. This is the simplest tack rope arrangement ;
but it is possible you may find that, instead of the
rope being fast to the boom, one end is attached to
a stout screweye on the thwart, from which the rope
leads through a (pulley) " block " attached to the
boom, and from there leads down to the hole in the
thwart and the cleat. This device of a block and a
doubled rope is called a " single whip purchase,"
and it pulls down the boom with a force that is
double the force your hand has exerted. It is, in
fact, a form of lever, the power of which can be

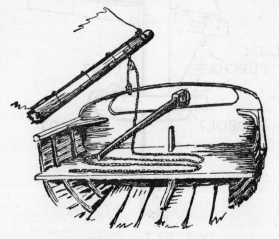

Fig. 9. Mainsheet with whip purchase and horse.

multiplied by winding a rope backwards and forwards over pulley sheaves.

A similar purchase will be found in the case of the

" sheet " (originally " sheet rope ") which is the rope that pulls in the boom or lets it swing out over the boat's side, as required. This is but rarely attached directly to the boom, a purchase being needed to halve the strain on one's hand.

The block through which the sheet is " rove " (threaded) is attached to the boom a foot or so from the latter's after end. The " standing part " (permanently fixed end) of the sheet is either attached to a stout screw-eye in the hog just forward of the stern seat or else to a metal ring or some form of closed hook sliding along a " horse " (raised horizontal rail) bolted to the top edge of the transom. The purpose of this latter arrangement is to bring the standing part of the sheet directly under the boom, so pulling the latter downwards and flattening the sail.

The " fall " (loose end) of the sheet, unlike the falls of the halliard and tack rope, has neither cleat nor belaying pin to which it can be fastened, even temporarily. This is because the helmsman should keep it in his hand, ready to ease it out and relieve the sail of wind pressure instantly, should an exceptionally hard puff " heel " (lean) the boat over so far that water threatens to come in over the side.

THE FIRST VENTURE

A VARNISHED dinghy, when brand-new is a delight
to the eye; but it takes very little rough handling
to scratch and bruise its glossy planking permanently.
A new sail is equally vulnerable, and will never set
with the correct gull's wing curve unless when first
used it is stretched very gently and evenly in all
directions. For these reasons it would be unwise to
buy a new boat before some experience has been
gained, and the absolute novice should hire or, if
that is not possible, buy a dinghy to which a few
extra scratches will make little difference.

Here, with regard to hireable boats, a note of
warning must be sounded: sometimes sailing boats
offered on hire are unreliable. This may sound
strange; but a sailing boat's gear needs constant attention. Boat proprietors are often short-handed, so bits
and pieces come loose and break, and repairs are
not undertaken so long as the gear is in any way
useable. Should a sail tear or a rope break while
the boat is on hire some proprietors might say,
with an air of reproof: "This boat ain't had
fair treatment," and expect compensation. The
reader need not be alarmed by the above revelation,
for he can always row home; but he must digest

the fact that occasionally hireable boats are not in a fit state to be sailed in strong winds or rough water.

No matter whether the boat in which you first go sailing is bought—of course, on some knowledgeable person's recommendation—or hired by the hour or day from a hire boat proprietor, before going out in her for the first time the mast, sail and ropes should be spread on the ground for inspection, just to see that the sail is not torn, the spars split, the ropes frayed, or the " laces " loose that hold the sail to the yard and boom. This last defect is more than probable, even if the sailing gear is sound and well looked after, because the laces, which are of " small stuff " (cordage of string size) shrink and stretch considerably with the weather, and the slack must frequently be taken up.

Unless a sail is pulled out hand-tight along the yard and boom, and prevented by the laces from sagging away from them, it will set baggily and be very inefficient. If the cords are at all loose untie them at the " peak " (top corner of the sail) and at the " clew " (aftermost lower corner). At each corner you will find that there are two separate cords—a " lashing " which goes several times through the ring in the corner of the sail and the hole in the end of the spar, and the lace which goes alternately through the eyelets on the edge of the sail and round the spar, from one end to the other of the latter.

To tighten the sail up, first loosen the lace, and pull the lashing tight. Tie this, and then, starting at the far end, tighten the lace, eyelet by eyelet, finally tying the end to the ring in the sail's corner, tucking in or cutting off the end of the cord for the sake of a tidy finish.

If you are only hiring a boat for an hour or two, this fiddling with lashings and laces may appear a waste of time. But it is not so, for even the most expert boat sailor cannot control a boat under a sagging, baggy sail.

Since it will be obvious to the boat proprietor that you are a beginner, it is likely that he or one of his assistants may suggest coming with you as an instructor. If, as is possible, you feel a complete lack of self-confidence, there will be a temptation to accept such an offer. However, to do so would be a mistake. Gaining self-confidence is more than half the battle in acquiring watermanship, and that confidence you can only attain by accepting full responsibility. Again, not everyone has the gift for instructing, and a couple of hours spent largely in watching a practised helmsman who could not explain how and why things were done in a sailing boat the way he did them might well leave you with nothing more than false and confused impressions.

Going out alone in a sailing dinghy for the first time you must expect to make mistakes ; but even should you capsize her it matters little, provided you can swim a few strokes. Dinghies are never hired out in dangerous waters—it would not pay—and you may be sure the boat's owner will cast an occasional eye in your direction in case you or the boat should come to harm.

It is to be hoped that on this your first venture the dinghy, when taken over, lies tied to a landing-stage where there are several feet of water. This is because the rudder of a sailing dinghy projects deeper down into the water than her keel by quite a foot, and it would complicate matters if you had to row out into deeper water first, and then hook the rudder on while the boat was drifting.

We will assume, then, that there is plenty of water, and so, as a first step, you " ship " (hook on) the rudder, and after pulling out its securing pin lower the C.B. till its lifting handle rests on the top of the C.B. case. Next, up-end the mast ; pull the traveller about half-way down it ; and " step " it (set it up) through the hole in the thwart with its foot in the mast step. At the first effort you are quite likely to step the mast incorrectly. Look up it and see that the fall of the halliard leaves the slot in the masthead on the port side. If not, lift the mast clear of the step again, revolve it in your hands, and replace it correctly.

Now see that the pair of iron rowlocks and the tiller are on board, and lay the oars, one on each side, across the thwarts with the blades forward, and the handles on the stern seat.

Finally, while it is on shore, loosely bundle the sail between its spars, tucking in the sheet and the tack rope ; and seeing that the tack end of the boom is forward, lay the sail in the boat on the starboard side of the mast.

It is now time to take notice of the direction of the wind, which from this point onwards is going to be the governing factor. You want the wind to be blowing towards you from over the bows, as that makes it easy for you to hoist the sail without it instantly filling with wind, and blowing out over the side. Next best is with the " wind on the beam " (crossing the boat), because though the sail will fill with wind it will not start driving the boat ahead till you pull the sheet in. The wind direction to avoid is from over the stern ; because as soon as you raised any of the sail the boat would forge ahead, tugging at her " painter " (bow rope) so hard that you could only " cast it off " (undo it) from the ring or post on the landing with considerable difficulty, and might damage the boat against the landing before you could steer away from it.

As long as there is not a strong water current forcing the boat's stern round towards the wind, you can push her round to face the latter. If, on the other hand, there should be a strong current tending to force the boat's stern round against the wind your best course is to tie her to the landing by both bow and stern, forcibly keeping her head to wind till the sail is set. You can loop the stern line over the rudderhead if there is nothing else to tie it to.

With the boat lying approximately bows to wind, held either by the painter alone or by the painter

and a stern rope, you can now " make " (set) sail.
To do so, first reeve the tack rope downwards
through the hole in the forward thwart on the
starboard side of the mast, and make it fast to its
cleat or pin with figure of eight turns, allowing a
lot of slack, that is—from 18 ins. to 2 ft. Next tie
one end of the sheet to the ring on the horse, if there
is one, or to the eyebolt in the dinghy's bottom, if
that is how she is fitted, and put a knot in the other
end of the sheet, so that it cannot " unreeve "
(unthread itself) from the block on the boom.

Owing to the nearly triangular shape of the
sail you will find that to hook the yard to the mast
traveller when the former is right down and resting
on the thwart, you would have to drag the sail right
forward. To obviate this, pull on the halliard with
your left hand till the traveller has run up the mast
shoulder-high, and then with your right hand raise
the yard and hook it on. Then heave away on the
halliard till the boom is lifted a foot above the
forward thwart, after which draw all the slack of
the halliard down through the hole in the thwart on
the port side of the mast and make it fast to its pin
or cleat in the following way : First wind it round
with a figure of eight turn ; then commence a
second turn and make a loop about 2 ins. long in the
free part of the halliard just beyond the last turn.
Tuck the loop under, so that it jams. (Fig. 10). This
is called a " slippery hitch," and its virtue is that
while it holds a rope firmly to its cleat or pin as long
as you do not touch it, yet by jerking the free end of

the fall you withdraw the loop, and can cast off the figure-of-eight in a second.

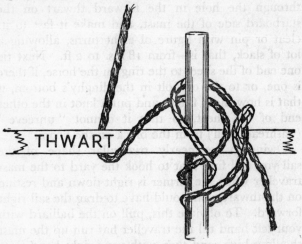

Fig. 10. The Slippery Hitch.

On hoisting the sail, as you have just done, you will find that the boom swings forward, its after end still lying in the stern of the dinghy. That after end must be raised sufficiently for you to be just able to dodge your head under it when sitting steering, so heave down the tack rope hard, and make it fast in the same way as you did the halliard, but, of course, on the starboard side. This will flatten the sail and lift the after end of the boom.

The sail is now set, but before casting off the shore lines, push the tenon of the tiller into its socket in the rudderhead, with the tiller under the loop of the stern line, should you be using one. Also, as this is your first sailing effort, and you may want to resort to the oars if you cannot get the boat to turn solely with the rudder, ship the rowlocks in the forward pair of rowlock sockets. Then, from where you sit steering, you can, any time it is necessary, give a pushing stroke with one or other of the oars to turn the bows to port or starboard.

In all probability, starting out from a hiring station, you will be able to get somebody to cast off your bow and stern lines and throw them on board. If not, jump ashore, and first untie the stern line, if there is one, and then the painter ; but keep hold of the latter till you are safely back in the boat, lest she sails away without you. Take the loop off the rudder-head and coil both lines away snugly as soon as you are clear of the landing. If the wind is pinning the dinghy against the landing use an oar as a boathook and shove off hard before pulling in the sheet and filling the sail. As soon as you are clear of the shore pull the sheet halfway in, with the rudder turn the boat till the wind is blowing across the boat and filling the sail, and settle yourself for steering, sitting on the side seat with your back to the wind, the tiller in one hand and the sheet in the other. The boat will now begin to forge ahead, her bows tending at the same time to head round against the wind. All sailing boats do this, and you check the turning tendency by pulling the tiller ever so slightly to windward.

No matter whether you wish to go up stream or

down, or whether the wind is blowing across your intended course, or with or against the stream, for the first few minutes you should sail with the wind " on the beam " also called " sailing on a reach," that is to say with the wind passing straight across the boat. This is the easiest " point of sailing " (course relative to the wind), and it will not make much difference should you be holding the sheet too far in or letting it too far out. Even though the wind may be light, you will find as soon as the wind fills the sail that it makes the boat " list " (lean) to leeward. A boat sails best leaning slightly ; but an open boat will, of course, fill with water if you let her lean far, and you must keep her as upright as you can by leaning back to windward. On her own account a dinghy has very little stability, so the weight of your body must be used to keep her upright. Whenever the wind strengthens, wedge your toes under the leeward side seat, and lean your shoulders well back over the " weather " (windward) gunwale to use your weight to the best advantage in keeping the boat upright.

Now that you are fairly " under way " (moving freely ahead) we will take it that you are reaching and " on the starboard tack " (with the wind coming from the starboard side). Sitting back to the wind you will have the tiller in your left hand and the sheet in your right. As your boat draws well away from the shelter of the shore probably the wind comes stronger, and you find that in spite of your leaning back to balance the boat she still tips over and her " lee " (leeward) gunwale looks as if it might easily dip under water. To counteract this, and bring her more nearly " on to an even keel " (upright) let a few inches of the sheet slip through the fingers of your right hand, so that the sail is less held in and " spills " (presents lessened resistance to) the wind. Only a few inches should be released, and that slowly, or the sail will flap uselessly, and the boat come upright with a jerk that might throw you backwards.

If, as well as steadily strengthening, the wind every now and then comes in a specially hard puff, you will want not only to relieve the sail by easing the sheet, but also by " luffing " (turning the bows more towards the wind). To do this " put down the helm " slightly (push the tiller away from you). This only means moving the handle end of it about one inch towards the port side of the boat for a few seconds while the hard puff lasts. If you were to push it further and keep it there the boat would head right into the wind and stop dead with the sail flogging uselessly. The boat would then be " in irons " (unsteerable) and you would have to turn her bows away from the wind with the oars before you could steer and sail her again.

After every such momentary puff of wind you should pull in the sheet again and " bear away " (pull the tiller back to where it was), so that the bows point more away from the wind, and the sail again takes the full wind force.

If on this occasion—your first sail—the wind

should rapidly strengthen to a really hard breeze it will be unfortunate, because one must have had considerable practice before one can cope with such conditions effectively. Under the present circumstances you need not be ashamed to make discretion the better part of valour, lower the sail and row in, whereas when you have got more used to sailing you will without further ado take in a reef and carry on. We may, however, assume that you have your due measure of beginner's luck, that the wind does not increase beyond a steady sailing breeze.

So far you have been sailing on a reach with the wind squarely crossing the boat. That, as has been said, is the easiest point of sailing, and after getting the " feel " (sense of control) of the tiller and sheet you should ease your pull on the tiller ever so slightly, so that the boat's bows point a little closer towards the wind, and then, as the sail begins to lose the wind and shake, pull in the sheet till the sail is again " asleep " (steadied by the wind).

The boat is now sailing " full and by," which means : on a course at less than a right angle to the wind's path, but yet not at the finest angle to the wind that the boat could follow. To find how " close to the wind " she can sail, let the tiller even slacker in your hand, and pull in the sheet till the boom is nearly over the centreboard case. The dinghy will now head within half a right angle of the wind's path, and you will feel it full on your cheek instead of on the back of your neck. Now the boat will be moving very slowly, the sail inclined to flutter ; and looking over the stern you will see that the eddies left behind in the water are streaming, not straight behind, but over the windward quarter. This latter is a sure proof that the boat, instead of sailing straight, is crabbing to leeward. This, of course, is very inefficient sailing, for you could follow the same track through the water with the sail further out to the side and the bows pointing at a wider angle from the wind's path, and you would then be travelling very much faster. Pull in the tiller a trifle, and slightly slack out the sheet ; you will then sail as fast as it is possible to sail to windward. The other way—with the sail right in—was " pinching the boat," and only worth trying so that you might observe the result of it.

Everybody, when first learning to steer, has a tendency to grasp the tiller firmly and hold it in a rigid grip as if otherwise it might jerk free. The tiller will do no such thing, and actually you should control it with a finger tip touch, when in consequence you will feel from its pressure against your hand just how much force is required to keep the boat straight. This is important ; because the rudder acts as a brake as well as serving to direct the boat, and so you want to bring it into action as little as possible. Particularly do you need to exercise a light touch when sailing to windward, because every now and then a stronger puff of wind will shoot the boat ahead and automatically turn her bows more towards the wind. This means a few extra yards gained in getting to windward, and you do not want to pull on the tiller and bring her back to her former course till the lightening of this helpful puff of wind makes it necessary in order that her speed may be maintained, and that the sail may not develop a flutter.

TACKING AND RUNNING

EXCEPT on the open sea, which is not the best place for a first sailing effort, because there are the complications of the waves and tidal currents, you will not be able to sail far in any direction without meeting the shore and having to turn. Then, if you have so far been sailing close hauled, to windward, you will have to " tack " (turn the bows to the wind, and keep the boat turning till the wind strikes the sail on the other side). This is also called " putting about."

We assumed at the outset that you left the shore sailing on the starboard tack, when the tiller would be in your left hand, the sheet in your right, and your back against the starboard gunwale as you sit across the boat. Now, as you approach the shore, you will have to turn the boat's bows to starboard, and bring the wind over the port bow, when the boat will come on to the port tack. This turn is, of course, made against the wind and through a full quarter of a circle, so the boat must be travelling fairly fast at the outset, or before she has finished the complete turn she will have stopped dead, with no further response to the rudder. For this reason you must first get her sailing at her best speed by

B   33

slightly pulling the tiller towards you and so making
her " pay off " (turn away from the wind to bring
it broad on the bow). Keep her on that course for
about ten seconds while she gathers speed, and then
" put the helm down " (push the tiller over towards
the leeward gunwale), taking two or three seconds
over this movement, and then keeping the tiller
there till the boat is right round on the port tack
with the wind on the port side of the sail. As the
sail now begins to fill with wind, let go of the tiller,
change your sitting position to the side seat on the
port side, change the sheet from your right hand to
your left, take the tiller in your right hand, and pull
it gently to prevent the boat heading back towards
the wind. Now you are sailing close-hauled on
the port tack and can carry on as before, leaving
the shore behind you.

In calm water and with a steady breeze you can
hardly fail to turn the boat from one tack to the
other if the above instructions are carried out. On
the other hand a gusty wind that keeps changing
direction may stop the boat in the middle of her
turning movement, and either put her back on to
her original tack or drive her sternwards, when she
will be impossible to steer. Steep waves can, and
often do, have the same effect.

If, having put down the tiller to turn the boat
from the starboard to the port tack, you see that,
owing to one or both of the above causes, she is not
fully responding, leave go of the sheet and tiller,
quickly drop an oar into the rowlock on the port

side, and with it give one or two steady pushing
strokes. This will keep the boat moving ahead and
turning to starboard. As soon as she has turned
far enough to bring the wind on to the port side
of the sail, drop the oar into the boat, pull the tiller
slightly towards you with your right hand and pull
in the sheet with the left.

In the case of most rivers and creeks, particularly
where the banks are high, the wind tends to follow
the channel rather than to blow across it from bank
to bank. As a consequence sailing in these narrow
waters is mainly confined to running down wind
in one direction, and in the other proceeding by
a series of short tacks from bank to bank. The
zigzag course followed by your boat is then several
times as long as the distance she " makes good "
to windward up or down the river. Under such
conditions you get as much sailing practice as on
broader waters, but you do not get much "for-
rarder."

" Running " (sailing down wind) many experienced sailing folk will assure you, is much
simpler for the helmsman than beating to windward,
and this is true to the extent that skilful helmsmanship does not result in any notable gain in speed,
as it does in the case of beating to windward. On
the other hand, if the wind is really strong and the
expanse of water sufficient for waves to form,
steering down wind becomes difficult, because the
boat tends to yaw to port and starboard, and also
to roll. Under such conditions steering a straight

course is by no means easy, and the problems involved must now be studied in detail.

Whilst beating to windward between the banks of the river you will have found that owing to the bends in the stream the wind did not everywhere follow its course exactly, but in some reaches blew across the river at a fine angle, with the result that on one tack you could nearly " lay your course " (follow the direct course you want to make good), remaining on the same tack for quite a time, whilst on the other tack you could only sail straight across to the opposite bank. This is called beating on a " long and short leg."

Now, if it was the case that in a certain reach of the river you were able to make a long leg on the starboard tack, the wind will have been blowing towards you from the shore ahead of you seen from over the starboard bow.

Then, should you decide to turn the boat round and run before the wind back to your starting point, and therefore pull the tiller to starboard, the following things will happen : as the boat circles to port the wind, from being on the starboard bow, will come first on the starboard beam and then on the starboard quarter ; still turning, she will next bring it right astern, and finally by the time she is heading in the desired direction it will be on her port quarter. This will involve you in pulling the sail round against the wind, a manoeuvre called " jibing," in which the sail and boom tend to go over—in this case to the starboard side—with a violent jerk, which in a strong wind may cause a capsize. That is why it is better to turn down wind from the short leg tack—in this particular case the port tack—so that you will still have the wind on the same side of the sail, though now reaching instead of beating. (Fig. 11).

In steering a boat under sail you will already have noticed that, whether you are reaching or

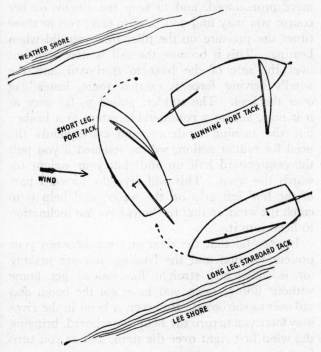

Fig. 11. The safe way of turning down wind.

beating to windward, she shows a constant tendency
to turn head to wind, a tendency one has to counter
by maintaining a slight pull on the tiller. This
tendency is called " carrying weather helm "
meaning that the helm or tiller has to be pulled
in the direction from which the " weather " (wind)
is coming. Now that you are running with the
wind on the port quarter this tendency becomes
more pronounced, and to keep the dinghy on her
course you may find you have to exert two or three
times the pressure on the tiller that you did when
beating. This is because the sail is now well out
over the side of the boat to starboard, and the
wind's driving force is exerted there, instead of
over the keel. The rudder, pulled so far over as
it is now, acts to a considerable extent as a brake ;
but the turning tendency, and consequently the
need for rudder action, will be lessened if you pull
the centreboard half up and shift your weight towards the stern. This will give the forward part
of the hull less grip on the water, and help it to
catch the wind, so that the bows have less inclination
to head into it.

It may be that the river or creek between your
present position and the landing you are making
for is sufficiently straight for you to get home
without jibing, once you have got the boom and
sail over to starboard. However, a bend in the river
may force you to turn the boat to starboard, bringing
the wind first right over the stern, and as you turn
further, over your starboard quarter.

This swinging of your stern round across the wind's path will, of course, involve jibing. But the violent jerking over of the sail can be mitigated if you watch the sail's behaviour and act accordingly. To begin with, as the boat comes stern to wind, there will be a bellying out of the middle of the sail, the boom will lift, and the boat will lurch and roll. Hauling in the sheet till the boom points over the starboard quarter will reduce this latter tendency, but as you turn the boat with the rudder still further the wind will come more and more from over that quarter, till suddenly the wind fills the sail on its starboard side. Provided that you do not let this shift of wind take you unawares, you can reduce the consequent jerk by gently paying out the sheet while keeping a check on it. On the other hand, if the sheet can go with a run and is then pulled up suddenly, there will be such a jerk that the boat may capsize. In a really strong wind this violent jerk is almost inevitable, so it is then much safer to turn the boat head to wind, and change tack, as already described.

That tendency to yaw and roll when running before a strong wind, to which we have referred, can be checked to some extent by pulling in the sheet till the boom is nearly over the quarter instead of square to the wind and at right angles to the boat's keel, its normal position in running. In a steady wind this should prove effective ; but a heavy gust is always liable to make the boat " sheer " wildly (sweep round towards the wind, away from her course), and this may result in a violent collision with the bank or with some other craft.

This tendency to " take charge " (refuse to steer straight) is a sure sign that too much sail is being carried for the strength of wind encountered, and that the time has come when the sail's exposed area must be reduced by reefing.

There are two ways of reefing a sail. One is to roll the lower part of it round the boom, like a window blind, and the other is to gather this portion of the sail into pleats, tying them into a long, thin bundle along the boom and on top of it by means of a row of short cords, called " reef points " that are sewn to the sail in pairs, one cord on each side of it. As can well be imagined, with suitable gear it is quicker and easier to roll away the lower part of a sail than to tie it into a bundle ; but the boom of a dinghy's lugsail cannot be satisfactorily fitted to revolve, and this type of sail is therefore provided with one or more rows of reef points, so located that you can dispose of 1 ft., 2 ft., or 3 ft. of sail area, as required. Each row of reef points is terminated at the luff and leach of the sail by " cringles," which are brass rings bound round with the roping on the edges of the sail, and these when tied down to the boom take the strain off the reef points.

One of the disadvantages of reef points for reducing a dinghy's sail is that you cannot satisfactorily bunch up and tie away the lower part of the canvas while the boat is sailing and the sail itself distended with wind—not even if there are two of you on board, and the other attends to the steering. The sail must first be lowered into the boat.

Were you to reach forward, loose the halliard from its cleat, and try to lower the sail while it was distended by a following wind there might be trouble ; for the mast traveller, pulled hard against the masthead by the yard, would not come down readily ; and when you had managed to pull the sail and its yard part way down, in all likelihood the wildly flapping sail would blow overboard. Because of this, never lower a dinghy's sail in a following wind, unless you have to in some such emergency, as when there is not room to turn, yet sail has got to be reduced immediately. Under all other conditions before lowering the sail, put down the tiller, pull in the sheet and so bring the boat's bows to the wind. Then, the sail being relieved, you cast loose the halliard and let the sail down with a run.

Once the sail is lowered snugly into the boat you can, if well away from the shore, just let the boat drift while you tie in the reef. On the other hand, your first effort at reefing will take ten minutes at the very least, and you do not want to be distracted by watching the boat's uncontrolled drift, or by having to use the oars to avoid obstructions. It is better to pull up the C.B., pull out the tiller, unship the rudder, and row to the bank

B*

where you can tie up, and set about this reefing business at leisure.

In tying down a reef there are three distinct operations : First, tying down the cringle that is on the luff opposite the lowest row of reef points, making it fast to the forward end of the boom. Second, pulling the cringle that is at the other end of the row of reef points, on the leach, as far as it will stretch towards the after end of the boom, where you tie it down, finally tying each pair of reef points round the boom. When a reef is "shaken out" (untied) the opposite order is observed. This is because if the sail was—even momentarily— held down solely by the reef points, any slight localised strain where the points are sewn on would be sufficient to tear the sail, which is only really strong along its roped edges.

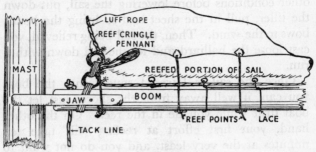

Fig. 12. A Reef tied down.

The tying down of the reef cringles to the boom is done with " reef pendants " (pronounced " pennants," pieces of cord 1 ft. to 2 ft. long). First reeve the luff pendant backwards and forwards two or three times between the luff cringle and the cringle in the corner of the sail at the tack ; pull the ends, drawing the two cringles together ; and finish by winding both ends in opposite directions round the boom, and tying them together with a reef knot. (Fig. 12.) If the pendant proves over-long tuck its ends into a fold of the sail so that they cannot " foul " (get mixed up and jam) the tack rope. Next, take hold of the leach reef cringle, making sure that it is the one at the end of the lowest row of reef points, and not the one in line with the second or third row. Pull it aft along the boom, and secure it to the cringle at the corner of the clew. You will find in this case that the two cringles do not meet, so finish up with several turns taken with the pendant ends through the reef cringle and round the boom, without their going through the clew cringle, before tying them together and tucking them away.

It is in this process of tying down a reef that the beginner, maybe for the first time, will be making reef knots so, though the making of a reef knot can be followed from the illustrations, a few words on the subject will not be out of place.

Any person not in the habit of handling cordage, if he wishes to tie two ropes' ends together, does so with a " grannie " knot ; because, after twisting the rope in his left hand once round the rope in his right hand, he tends automatically to continue twisting and bring it behind the one in his right

(Fig. 13a.), finally pushing the same tip through the loop so formed and completing the knot. Instead, to make a reef knot, the end of the left-hand rope is brought across the front of the rope in your right hand, taken round the back of it, and brought through towards you. (Fig. 13b).

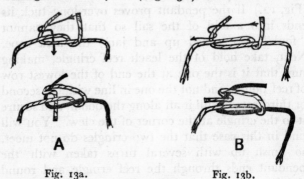

Fig. 13a.   Fig. 13b.

The reason why you should always use a reef knot for boat work and never a grannie, is that while both hold securely, only the former is readily untied, and the ability to free a rope quickly is very often of the utmost importance. The fact that they are easily untied is the particular virtue of the whole range of seamen's knots.

When you have tied the luff and leach cringles to the boom at either end, the " bunt " (part away from edges) of the sail below the first row of reef points should be neatly pleated into small folds along the top of the boom and there secured with the reef points. These latter are in pairs, one on either side of the sail. Pass one of them under the boom and tie the pair together with a reef knot at the side of the boom ; which side does not signify as long as all the knots come on the one side, so that untying them again is easy. It matters little which pair of points is tied first, but the neatest job will result if you commence at mid-length and work forward and aft alternately.

The first time you tie a row of reef points you will, of course, not want to complicate the ordinary reef knot ; but should the thin cord of the reef points be wet, even a reef knot may prove difficult to untie. When you have reached the stage of being able to tie this knot without thinking, make a practice of bending double the end which you push through as a final movement. This makes it a

PULL TO UNTIE

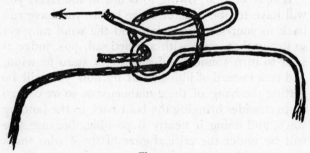

Fig: 14

single bow, which can instantly be loosened by a jerk on the very end (Fig. 14).

The sail, after the reef has been tied down,

should be set in just the same way as you set it when starting out. Coil down the sheet on the stern seat, loosely make fast the halliard and the tack rope to their respective pins or cleats, so that they will be to hand ; push out from the shore, head to wind, with the oars, till there is water enough under the boat for you to lower the C.B., and ship the rudder ; push the tiller back into the rudder-head, hoist the sail quickly and bowse down the tack rope before the bows have time to " pay off " (blow away down wind). Now that the sail is once more set, you can pull in the sheet till the sail fills with wind, and head the boat down wind by pulling the tiller to windward. In spite of the reduction in sail area you will find the boat not much slower, but, on the other hand, a great deal easier to steer.

It may be that, owing to bends in the river, you will have to jibe once or twice before you have run back to your starting point, and the wind may get so strong that, even with a reefed sail, you judge it safer to turn round head instead of stern to wind, and tack instead of jibing ; but by now you will be getting the hang of these manoeuvres, so we can go on to consider bringing the boat back to the landing stage, and doing it neatly if possible, because you will be under the critical gaze of those who think they could have done it ever so much better themselves !

Should the wind be really strong—strong enough to blow your cap off unless you cram it down hard

—you had better make discretion the better part of valour by rounding up head to wind right away from the landing, lowering your sail, and rowing in. That is not timidity, it is seamanship, for an over-powering gust of wind might strike the sail at the last critical moment, causing the boat to ram the landing and break her stem.

Ordinarily, coming in before the wind, you should run on past the landing for a matter of ten yards, and then beat back towards it. Finally, you should lower the sail when a boat's length off, and steer her in under her remaining impetus, so that she just grazes the string plank, and you can jump ashore with the painter in your hand.

There is only one occasion when you should run down wind straight at a landing, and that is when the wind is so weak and an adverse current so strong that the boat barely creeps " over the ground " (moves forward in relation to the land). Then you can run straight in ; but pull in the boom so that it does not foul the jetty or other boats, and lower the sail carefully into the boat at the last instant before she touches the landing.

On this, the first occasion of your bringing a sailing boat in to a landing stage, you are almost certain to misjudge the amount of "way" (momentum) the boat carries over the last few yards of your approach, whether up wind or down. Indeed, even a thoroughly practiced boat sailor may make a mistake in this if handling a strange boat, for some stop almost dead under circumstances where others will continue on their way for two or three times their own length after the sail is lowered, depending on their weight and hull form. In any case, make a point of lowering the sail too early rather than too late ; for it is better to have to finish up under oars, than to come tearing into a fleet of moored boats, creating a scene of devastation.

CHAPTER IV

DYNAMICS APPLIED TO SAILING

So commonplace is the sight of light objects blown along by the wind that we never consider how an air current's energy is transferred to a solid body ; yet that is something which one must first comprehend to employ sails to full advantage. Wind energy is momentum, the product of weight and speed. The weight of the air is practically constant, but its speed is extremely variable.

When air in motion encounters the yielding sail it gives up some of its momentum to the latter, is itself deflected, and goes on its way with reduced velocity.

As the dinghy with her lugsail has shown, the sail must be adjusted at various angles to the wind's path according to the course relative to the wind she is desired to take ; but in every case there is another condition, not so far referred to, that has to be fulfilled : the air that has done its work, energising the sail, must be induced to escape, so that further, faster-moving air may without hindrance constantly take its place.

That need was not recognised before the age of science. Our ancestors used baggy sails to entrap the wind, and caught a lot of useless eddies. Now,

with a clearer understanding of fluid mechanics we
form our sails as curved vanes, the curvature being
variable to meet the conditions of beating, reaching
and running.

The direction and some suggestion of the amount
of energy the wind can be made to yield are shown
diagramatically in Fig. 15.

First consider the simple case of reaching with a
beam wind, which this diagram represents. The
bent arrow ABC indicates the direction of the air
currents before and after contact with the sail, on
striking which they lose some of their velocity and
are deflected sternwards, while they push the sail
in the direction BD.

Now just as the reaction of AB together with BC
is the single thrust BD, so this latter is resolvable
into two forces acting in separate directions, namely
DE and DF. This resolving of one force into two
is familiar to everybody in the splitting of wood
with a steel wedge. You drive in the wedge
edge-on, and acting in two directions it splits the
wood into two portions, forcing them aside to left
and right.

But, to return to our air currents—the force DF,
which is pressing the sail, and the boat with it,
sideways to leeward, is opposed and largely absorbed
by the resistance of the centreboard to sideways
movement. The other force, DE is not resisted by
the centreboard, which is edge on to it. This force
therefore is free to push the boat ahead, acting,
not where it is shown for clearness, right clear

of the boat, but at B, against the sail's central surface.

The case of a boat beating to windward with her sail trimmed close in is similar in general principle to the above ; but it differs in the proportion of the wind's energy that can be applied to driving

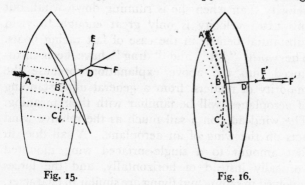

Fig. 15.   Fig. 16.

the boat forward. In Fig. 15 it will be noted that there are six rows of dots representing the column of moving air which impinges on the sail, and in Fig. 16 there are only three rows of such dots, indicating a narrower column, because the sail in this latter case presents a narrower front to the wind, and can only absorb energy to a diminished extent. Again, in Fig. 15, the lines DE and DF are equal, whilst in Fig. 16 DE representing the " lift " factor, is much shorter than DF, the " drag " factor, and the energy in each case is in proportion to the length of these lines.

Taking these facts together, it will be appreciated

how little of the wind force can be applied to driving a boat forward when she is sailing close hauled ; so that on this point of sailing she is much slower than when reaching or running. Since she is travelling to some extent up the wind's path, the effective or relative wind strikes the sail with a little more velocity than when she is running down wind, but this extra velocity is only great enough to yield substantial benefit in the case of fast racing boats. The words " lift " and " drag " have been introduced into the above explanation, because the majority of readers, from a general understanding of aeroplanes, will be familiar with their meaning. The wind acts on a sail much as the relative wind acts on the wing of an aeroplane. A sail does in fact amount to a single-surfaced wing mounted vertically instead of horizontally, and the forces involved in sailing and flying are similar in character, though very different in intensity. The pressure on a sail is rarely more than 2 lb. per square foot, whilst that on an aeroplane's wing amounts to 20 lb. and more in some cases.

While we are on this subject—comparing sails with aeroplanes' wings—the reader's notice may be drawn to the striking resemblance between the tall, narrow Bermudian sail, which both racing yachts and cruisers carry, and the wing of a monoplane.

From the spar-making, rigging and sail-making points of view the Bermudian sail is much more troublesome than a lug sail or any other sail that is relatively broad and set on a shorter mast ; because of the difficulty of holding up straight such a tall, thin mast, and of setting such a narrow strip of sail cloth at a fair curve all the way up.

These are admitted defects, but the advantage of this sail lies in its very long luff, corresponding to the wing's leading edge ; for it is the area just aft of the luff or leading edge that produces most of the lift in a wing or the windward propulsion in a sail. Moreover, the tip of a wing or peak of a sail is inefficient, because the air can spill round it instead of all sweeping across to the trailing edge or leach ; so the taller your sail or the longer your wing, the greater its proportion of efficient to inefficient area. One of the defects of the biplane is that it suffers from having four wing tips in place of the monoplane's two. The same defect is present in all yacht and boat rigs with more than one sail.

Reverting to the subject of masts, it will be realised that a tall vertical spar must set up a great deal of resistance or " drag," and break the wind flow into eddies at the luff of the mainsail. This is a grave disadvantage, and all sorts of expedients have been tried to reduce the drag and eddy formation. Masts of square and triangular cross-section have been tried, also masts of streamlined section ; but there is no benefit obtainable unless an edge can be presented to the wind on both tacks, and that can only be done with a mast revolving on its axis, an arrangement which complicates the rigging and mast fittings. Double-surfaced sails, enclosing the mast, cut out the eddies behind the latter ; but, of course, such sails are heavier than ordinary single-surfaced sails, and the two thicknesses of sailcloth are bound to chafe each other where they come in contact. To some slight extent lugsails get over the difficulty, the mast standing away from the luff of a lugsail on one tack ; but when on the other tack, the sail is pressed by the wind against the mast, and the latter makes a ridge down the sail which completely upsets its wing curvature.

The great difference between the speed of the wind acting on a sail and that of the relative wind acting on a wing must always be borne in mind when sails and wings are compared, otherwise—like many a sailing pundit—you will arrive at false conclusions.

As specific cases of a similarity in character, but not in degree, we may take the three factors in wing performance : upper surface vacuum, slot action, and biplane interference. Each of these has a counterpart in reference to sails ; the first affects all sails, and the other two can occur wherever there is a jib affecting the air flow past a mainsail.

Taking the first—upper surface vacuum—it is recognised than an aeroplane wing receives more lift from the reduction of normal air pressure due to a partial vacuum over its upper surface than it does from the increased air pressure over its under surface. This partial vacuum is caused by the fast moving edge of the wing ploughing up the air and shooting it in a wave over its back, leaving a hollow

over the wing's upper surface. A sail, with only
one twentieth the speed, only does this to a minor
extent, and the lift of the " upper " or leeward
surface, though a help, cannot be expected to exceed
the lift received by the " lower " or windward
surface.

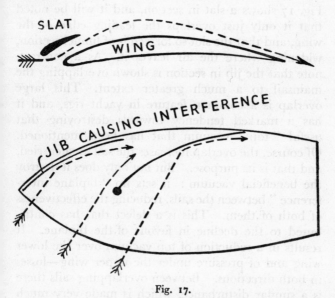

Fig. 17.

Slot action, of which the airman takes advantage
to prevent an aeroplane from an excessive angle of
incidence, when the nose of the aeroplane is thrown
up to check its speed or steepen its climb, is of considerable importance in a sailing boat. In the case
of an aeroplane the slot is an air gap formed between

a narrow aerofoil, called a " slat," and the leading edge of the wing. In a boat the headsail acts as a slat, it being in front of the mainsail. Both slat and headsail perform as wind guides, steadying the flow of air over the back of the wing or sail, so that the air current does not break up into eddies. Fig. 17 shows a slat in section, and it will be noted that it only just overlaps the leading edge of the wing, and that the slot so formed is of funnel section, widening where the air leaves it. As a contrast, note that the jib in section is shown overlapping the mainsail to a much greater extent. This large overlap is a common feature in yacht rigs, and it has a marked tendency towards destroying that useful " top " vacuum that has been mentioned. Of course, the overlap increases the sail area carried, and that is its purpose. But not only does it destroy the beneficial vacuum ; it sets up " biplane inter-ference " between the sails, reducing the effectiveness of both of them. This is a defect that has contri-buted to the decline in favour of the biplane. It results in a reduction of top vacuum over the lower wing and of pressure under the upper wing—losses in both directions. Between overlapping sails there is a similar disturbance, which is made very much worse if the headsail is sheeted in more closely than the mainsail ; for then the wind is trapped between the leach of the headsail and the luff of the mainsail, and neither sail can draw effectively.

So far, for the sake of simplicity in dealing with the wind's general action on a sail the latter has in the main been treated as if it were a blade or foil supported perpendicularly, and trimmed at a constant angle to the wind from foot to peak so that the wind sweeps horizontally across it from luff to leach. In practice the conditions are never as simple as that. First, there is the " listing " (leaning over) of the boat under wind pressure, and again, the upper part of the leach of a sail always sags away from the wind, because it is held in by the sheet to a less extent than is the sail's foot. The sail is therefore twisted.

Listing causes the wind to follow an upward, diagonal path across the sail, and by reaction the sail is pressed downwards rather than forwards. Moreover, the greater part of the sail then lies to leeward of the hull, instead of over it, and it tends to turn the boat round to windward, just in the same way as one of a pair of propellors turns a ship out of her course if the other propellor stops. To counteract this turning tendency you have to use the rudder all the time, and that reduces the boat's speed considerably.

With regard to the second factor, the twisting away from the wind of the upper portion of the leach of a sail, the claim is commonly made that this is beneficial when a boat is sailing close hauled to windward, because the wind up there, clear of the water, is stronger than lower down, and the stronger the wind the further can a sail be eased off, and so gain more " lift " or forward propulsion with a reduction of drift to leeward. In the case

of really tall sails, thirty and more feet high, this is
no doubt true ; but in the instance of a small
boat's sail, with no area to speak of more than
fifteen feet above water, the difference in wind
strength is obviously insignificant, and therefore
the gain, if any, is trifling, and the twist should be
as slight as possible.

Most small boats' sails tend to twist far too much,
and so, to bring the head of their sails to a fine
enough angle to use the wind, you will see helmsmen
pulling in their sheets till their booms are central,
and the lower portions of their sails can produce
nothing but leeward drift. The remedy is to heave
down the tack as hard as you can without stretching
the sail out of shape, and where it is made possible
by the type of sail and its gear, to strain the head
of the sail forwards while giving a downward pull
on the sheet, so as to keep the leach stiff under
up-and-down tension.

We now come to the subject of the wind's action
on a sail when a boat is running before the wind, a
subject in which we are not helped by the study
of aeroplane or birds' wings, which do not have to
meet the air at right angles. In this case more is
to be learnt from the action of parachutes.

Whether a sail is trimmed for beating to windward
or for running free it is equally necessary that the
spent wind shall escape freely from its surface and
make way for a constant supply of air travelling
at its full velocity. When the sail is trimmed to
the wind either for beating close hauled or for

reaching with the wind crossing the boat the spent air escapes readily from the sail's leach, because there is a steady flow across the sail from the luff. A following wind, on the other hand strikes the sail perpendicularly, and is inclined to flow towards all the edges of the sail, like water overflowing the edge of a bucket. This causes turbulence and obstructs the on-coming air ; so it is of advantage to help the spent air to escape, and a slight slackening of a main halliard is sometimes of use in promoting a free passage for the air round the upper part of the mainsail's leach.

Spinnakers, which are baggy triangular sails used only for running free (Fig. 18), at one time were provided with holes in the middle, as are parachutes, to let the air escape that way. This was moderately effective ; but the up-to-date spinnaker is so cut and set as to induce a downward air flow, the wind finally escaping under the sail's foot. This lifts the boat's bows, whereas earlier spinnakers were inclined to bury them.

The spinnaker is a class of sail it is not proposed to deal with in any detail here, because spinnakers are most difficult to handle, and nobody should try setting one in a small open boat until he is far beyond his novitiate. The spinnaker is always set opposite the mainsail, with its foot extended by a light boom, which is pivoted to the forward side of the mast. With the mainsail extended over one side of the boat and the spinnaker over the other the centre of the total sail spread is brought in line

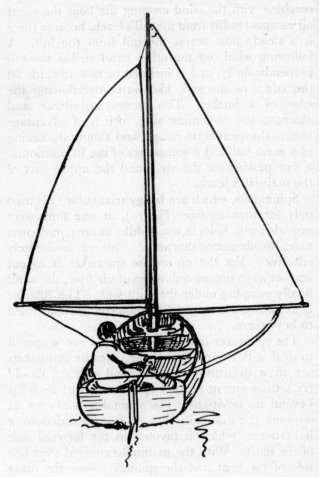

Fig. 18.

with the mast, so the boat sails straight down wind
on a steady course with scarcely any need for the
rudder's corrective use. Difficulties arise with a
spinnaker when the wind is not dead aft, but from
over the quarter. Then this sail sometimes fails
to receive and discharge the wind in a steady
flow, in consequence, wobbling so violently that
unless quickly and skilfully brought under control
or lowered into the boat it may upset her or break
the mast.

That is why it is no sail for beginners.

In this chapter reference has already been made
to that component of the wind's force which tends
to push the boat sideways to leeward, her consequent
drift being opposed by the centreboard. That is
the latter's sole purpose—it does not constitute
ballast—and the same result could be achieved
with a fixed fin, bolted below the keel, though the
latter would be troublesome in shallow water, and
make beaching the boat impossible.

Such devices as these two greatly reduce the
leeward drift, but they do not eliminate it, and a
boat sailing close hauled must be expected to follow
an actual course some ten degrees to leeward of her
apparent one.

When out sailing one aims at some landmark to
windward, it is necessary to head for the weather
side of it, so as to make up for this drift. If that
involves pointing the boat's stem too close to the
wind, one can only arrive off the landmark by
tacking. Just how far the boat is off her apparent

course will be seen on glancing astern. Were she
" following her nose " the wake would stream
straight aft from her rudder ; but owing to her
leeward drift you will find it away out over the
windward quarter.

For the best results in checking leeway a centreboard should be as deep as is practical, and its
width need not be greater than one-third of its
depth. The more deeply a centreboard is immersed
the more it cuts through " solid " water, which
cannot escape round its edges as readily as can
water nearer the surface.

Small boats' centreboards are usually made of
flat steel plate, sharpened at the edges. Wooden
or cast metal centreboards are also used, and these
can be of streamlined section, which makes them
more effective and less resistant to forward progress.
It is usual nowadays for a pair of sheet rubber lips
to be fitted to the boat's keel, one on each side of
the slot where the centreboard emerges. This cuts
out some of the water drag occasioned by the slot,
but the main purpose is to exclude stones and mud
from the centreboard case.

As long as the boat is forging ahead briskly her
centreboard will do its work ; but as she slows down
it becomes less and less effective. That is why
when sailing to windward you must not " pinch "
the boat, trying to sail too close to the wind and
losing its drive. Keep the boat forging ahead with
her sails full of wind, even though she then points to
leeward of the intended course. This gives the

centreboard a chance to function, and results in the best actual course to windward.

In choppy water you need to head the boat further away from the wind than is necessary under smooth conditions, because the short, steep waves absorb more of her driving force. Under such conditions do not head within half a right angle of the wind's path. Fifty degrees is nearer the mark, and you may then hope to follow an actual course not more than sixty degrees off the wind. That does not sound by any means " close to the wind " ; but it is as close as a small centreboard boat will usually sail under open sea conditions.

CHAPTER V

GUNTER LUGSAILS AND JIBS

THE practice and self-confidence gained from a few hours sailing in a lugsail dinghy, backed by a general understanding of the principles involved, should enable the reader to cope with a two-sailed boat after an even shorter spell of actual sailing in her than he required to learn to handle the lugsail.

Usually open boats with two sails are larger than those with one, and the handling of two sails in a dinghy less than 12 ft. long is rendered very awkward by the general lack of room. If possible, hire a rather heavy, beamy boat about 15 ft. long.

A boat of this size affords plenty of working space, so the halliards and sheets can be coiled where they will not be trod upon and tangled. If she is heavy her movements and general behaviour will not be too skittish for a beginner, who is likely to fumble with the gear and be somewhat slow in his handling of the jib sheets.

Not uncommonly hiring boats of this size carry a standing lugsail, such as you have already used, together with a jib. This latter, a small triangular sail in front of the mast is, in connection with two-sail rigs, sometimes called a " foresail." But, strictly, a foresail is a second triangular sail, carried between the jib and the mast in larger craft. In any case, both of these sails set forward of the mast are " headsails."

If this 15 ft. boat has a lugsail, there is only one special point to note, namely, that it must be set up with a tight halliard and tack rope, or it may sag forward and, with the lower end of its yard, foul the jib.

We will, however, assume that this boat carries a " gunter lug," a very effective sail, which the reader may later on favour for his own boat.

This sail is a latterday development from the " sliding gunter," a sail which was popular during the first half of last century. The sliding gunter was tall and triangular, in fact, much like the modern Bermudian sail in general appearance. However, in those days there was a very strong feeling against tall masts, and two thirds of the front edge of the sail was attached to a vertical spar, the " gunter yard," which slid up and down the back of a fairly short mast, being attached to it with " gunter irons."

These irons were shaped approximately as figures-of-eight. They were permanencies on the yard ; but the top one opened and the lower one was hinged, so that the spar and the head of the sail could be lowered horizontally down into the boat. The latching and unlatching of the upper iron round the mast was troublesome in a breeze, and both irons had a tendency to bind on the mast instead of sliding freely ; so in time a pair of open

C

jaws took the place of the lower iron, and various means were employed for keeping the yard vertical when it was hoisted. Some of these devices will be dealt with later ; but in a hiring boat probably you

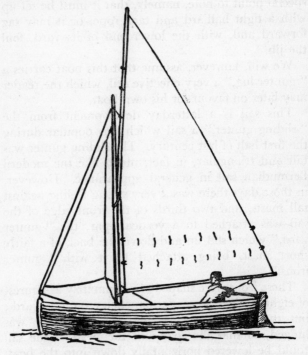

Fig. 19. The Gunter Lugsail

will find that there is nothing but a halliard, attached about halfway up the yard, serving both to hoist it, and to hold it close to the head of the mast. (Fig. 19).

Although this spar along the head of the sail is termed a " yard," and the present-day sail itself is spoken of as a " gunter lugsail ", these are misleading terms ; for this yard is in character a gaff, having at its foot jaws that slide on the mast, and the sail does not project forward of the mast in the characteristic lugsail manner.

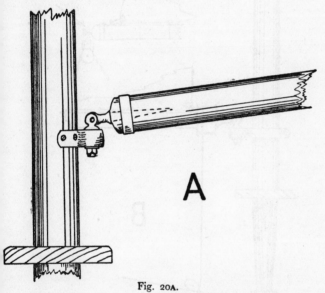

A

Fig. 20A.

As the sail is behind the yard and the yard behind the mast the lower front edge of the sail, comprising the luff, also lies behind the mast. It follows from this that the forward end of the boom must do the same, or there would be a twist in the luff of the sail. The forward end of the boom is either attached to the mast with jaws, like the yard, or with a "goose-neck," which is a form of universal joint. There are plain goose-necks (Fig. 20A), and goose-

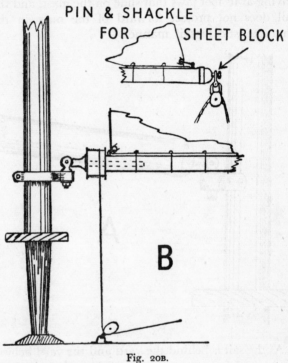

PIN & SHACKLE FOR SHEET BLOCK

B

Fig. 20B.

necks so fitted that the boom can be rotated by a wire rope and reel (Fig. 20B), or by a ratchet and hand lever, for reefing the sail round the boom like a roller blind. If the goose-neck is plain, you can only reef the sail with reef points and pendants, after the manner described in connection with a lugsail.

In view of the slowness and trouble of reefing with points and pendants, and the quickness and ease of rolling a sail round the boom, the latter system is much to be preferred ; and as the beginner is sure to encounter roller gear, if not in this second boat then in some other, at this point it had better be described in detail.

Were the boat larger, in all probability the boom would be revolved by a hand lever and ratchet or by a worm wheel, but being so small we may count on her having a plain reel or drum on the forward end of the boom having a thin flexible wire rope or a stout plaited cord wound round it and led through a block below the goose-neck to a cleat within the helmsman's reach. The fact of the boom revolving prevents the sheet being fastened to it anywhere but at the end, for otherwise it would roll up inside the sail. Not only has it to be at the extreme end, but free to swivel round a fixed pin. As it is the rotation of the boom that rolls the sail, the latter must be fixed to the boom in such a way that it cannot slip back. This is assured by fitting the rope that is sewn along the foot of the sail into a groove running along the boom, and holding it there by means of a " spline " (very thin and narrow wooden batten) screwed to the boom and overlapping the groove, so that the foot rope cannot be pulled out. A roller boom is a very simple device, yet it needs care in operation, or the sail will roll unevenly, and get pulled out of shape. To operate it, first detach 2 ft. to 3 ft. of the luff of the sail from the mast, if it happens to be laced to it. Then take the halliard in one hand and pay it out, keeping a moderate strain on it, while you pull strongly on the roller line with the other. The sail is thus kept flat as it descends, and should roll up smoothly. Finally, make fast the halliard and roller line, and take up the slack of the luff lacing.

That completes the reef, but there is yet a further adjustment you may have to make, for the point where the halliard is attached to the yard will now be well below the mast-head, and the yard may droop away from the mast in consequence. At the first favourable opportunity lower the yard, and shift the halliard up it so that the point of attachment is again opposite the sheave in the mast-head and will hold the yard upright. (Fig. 21).

Even the very smallest sailing dinghies are sometimes fitted with a jib as well as a mainsail, the intention being to produce that slot effect, which was dealt with in the preceding chapter. However, a jib has two sheets, both of which have to be adjusted on changing tack, and in the confines of an 8—10 ft. dinghy this can be very troublesome. In a 15 ft. boat there is plenty of room, and the fitting of a jib enables a smaller and handier mainsail to be used.

In a boat of this latter size the jib may be rigged

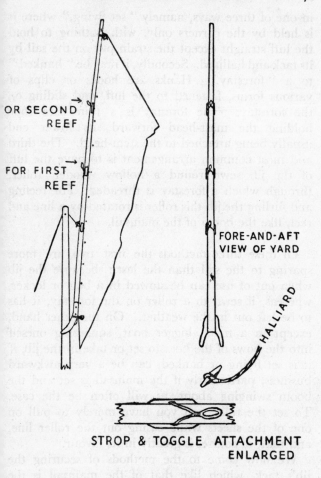

OR SECOND REEF

FOR FIRST REEF

FORE-AND-AFT VIEW OF YARD

HALLIARD

STROP & TOGGLE ATTACHMENT ENLARGED

Fig. 21. A Gunter Yard and its fittings.

in one of three ways, namely " set flying," where it
is held by the corners only, with nothing to hold
the luff straight except the strain put on the sail by
its tack and halliard. Secondly, it may be " hanked "
to a " forestay." Hanks are hooks or clips of
various forms, fastened to the luff, and sliding on
the forestay. The forestay is a thin wire rope
holding the mast-head forward, its lower end
usually being attached to the stem-head. The third
and most common arrangement is to have the luff
of the jib sewn round a hollow wooden roller,
through which a forestay is threaded. For reefing
and furling the jib this roller is rotated by a line and
reel, like the boom of the mainsail.

Of these three methods the first two are more
sparing to the sail than the last ; because the jib
when out of use can be stowed in a bag or locker,
whereas, if sewn to a roller on the forestay, it has
to be left out in the weather. On the other hand,
except in a much bigger boat, squeezing oneself
into the bows of the boat to set or take in the jib, if
it is set flying or hanked, can be a very awkward
business, particularly if the mainsail is set and the
boom swinging about, as will often be the case.
To set the roller sail you have merely to pull on
one of the sheets while easing out the roller line,
and that, of course, is greatly in its favour.

We now come to the methods of securing the
jib's tack, which like that of the mainsail is the
forward bottom corner. Whether this is held down

independently, or via a roller and stay, it will either be shackled to the stem-head or else extended beyond the bows of the boat and hooked to an iron " bumkin." This bumkin is a stout iron rod about 2 ft. long welded on to a stirrup which fits over the stem-head, being held there with a pin. The outer end of the bumkin has a hook on top for the tack and an eye underneath to which is attached a thin rod, the lower end of this in turn being shackled to the boat's stem at the waterline. (Fig. 22).

The pair of jib sheets which, united at the clew of the sail, are led, one each side, along the gunwales to cleats within reach of the helmsman, are usually a single piece of small rope with a loop at mid-length, which is furnished with a spring hook, a toggle and loop, or other attachment to the cringle in the clew of the sail. Whatever the form of this attachment, it has to be strong, as the occasional flapping of the jib will snap off any but the most secure contrivance.

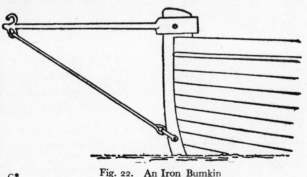

Fig. 22. An Iron Bumkin

Giving the exactly correct " lead " to the sheets by passing them through " fairleads " (guide rings) attached at carefully found locations on the gunwales is important ; but in a hired boat you will have to trust to them being in the right positions. If they are so, the jib will pull out into a fair winglike curve ; but if not, the sail will bag and shake at the edges. Put a large knot in the end of each sheet if there is not one already ; because otherwise the sheets are liable to get jerked by the sail sufficiently to unthread from the fairleads.

CHAPTER VI

MOORINGS, AND HANDLING HEADSAILS

Boats small and light enough for two men to lift on to a pontoon, or draw up a beach are usually kept out of the water when not in use, because all wooden craft soak up water to an extent which makes them noticeably heavier if they are afloat all the time.

However, a 15 ft. boat with sailing gear and a heavy steel centreboard may take four men to lift her out on to a pontoon or up a river bank ; so when you come to hire your first boat that is larger than the average dinghy and has a two-sail rig, it is more than likely that you will be rowed out to her in the boat proprietor's tender and find her lying to a mooring just clear of the fairway.

The class of mooring of which you have probably seen most up till now will have been ships' moorings, with large steel buoys, having rings to which ships are moored with wire ropes or chain. Small craft moorings are quite different from these and differently used ; so at this point we may digress from pure sailing matters and deal with the subject of mooring and unmooring a boat prior to your putting this into practice.

In those few yacht anchorages where there is plenty of room, and a boat can swing round a circle of, say, 50 ft. radius without risk of a collision with other craft, a mooring may have at the bottom end of its chain a single anchor, a block of stone, or some large piece of scrap-iron to hold the mooring in place. That, however, is rare in tidal yacht anchorages, which are usually very crowded, and most moorings, to restrict the boat's movements, have a pair of such anchors or weights, called "clumps," spread apart by a distance of as much as 100 ft. (Fig. 23), and united by a heavy ground chain or "bridle," to the middle of which is shackled

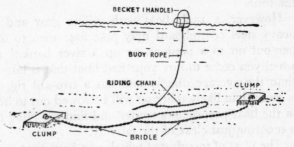

Fig. 23. A Yacht's Mooring.

a shorter length of thinner chain, called a "riding chain." This latter is the piece that is hauled aboard and made fast to the boat. Sometimes there are a number of riding chains attached at intervals to one bridle or ground chain. This type of boat mooring is called a "trot."

So far a boat mooring may sound a simple

contrivance and easy to use, but in practice, before you can get hold of the riding chain you have got to take on board the small cork or metal buoy that marks the mooring's position, and haul in the long length of rope attached to it, which in turn is fastened to the riding chain. The beginner's mistake, to which I wish to draw attention, is that of tying his boat to this rope or to the buoy, instead of hauling in the riding chain and making that fast, as he is meant to do.

Leaving even a light dinghy tied to a mooring buoy or its rope can cause a lot of trouble ; because these buoy ropes get rotten from their continuous immersion, and sometimes are no stronger than string. Of course, if the rope should break the boat will go adrift. No only that, it will take two men with a boat and a grapnel an hour or more to recover the riding chain. Therefore remember : when picking up a mooring lift the buoy on board, haul in the rope gently and coil it down. This will bring to hand the end of the riding chain, which you make fast to the mooring cleat in the bows, if there is one, or round the foot of the mast if there is not.

In unmooring a boat, first see that the rope is clear to run overboard unhindered. Then free the chain, and lower it into the water. Next, pay out the rope hand over hand after the chain, and finally throw the buoy overboard as the boat begins to gather way.

Now that we have detailed the process of mooring

and unmooring, it is time to describe the pre-
liminaries of getting under way with our comparatively large two-sailed boat, in which you will have
room to take a friend as crew, if you wish to do so.

In this connection, however, discretion may prove
the better part of sociability. It would be a
handicap to have anyone aboard who, thinking
himself the more experienced, insisted on taking
charge, or on laying down the law when you were
at the tiller. If you decide to take a companion,
choose another beginner, with whom you can
change places, each spending part of the time as
skipper and part as crew.

The skipper's job—steering, and tending the
mainsheet—now presents no novelty, and you can
carry on as in the one-sailed dinghy if you have a
crew ; for he tends the jib sheets, raises or lowers
the centreboard, and under the skipper's direction
attends to any part of the gear which cannot
readily be reached by the helmsman.

Having a crew is, of course, a considerable help ;
but sailing such a boat as this one single-handed is
not at all difficult, and it is well to get into the way
of doing so as soon as possible.

For the reasons already given, on boarding this
boat at her mooring you will find the riding chain
made fast forward in the boat, with the rope and
buoy on the bottom boards, somewhere by the foot
of the mast. Your first job now, as in the lugsail
dinghy, is to give the gear a look-over, seeing that
the sail lacings are set up on the yard and boom,

the various ropes attached, and nothing likely to
get caught or tangled during the process of setting
sail. If the boat is where she can float at low tide,
you are likely to find the rudder and tiller already
shipped. The gunter mainsail, too, is probably
ready for hoisting ; but the jib, unless on a roller,
may be stowed in a canvas bag or a stern locker, to
be out of the way of the wet and weedy buoy rope,
in which case you will have to get it ready for setting.

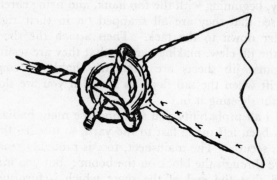

Fig. 24. A Sheet Bend

To do this, open it up, and make certain which of
its three corners are the tack, head and clew respec-
tively. Then hook or shackle the tack to the outer
end of the bumkin, if there is one, or to its alternative
—a ring or hole at the stemhead. The jib halliard
you will find rove through a block near the masthead. Make fast to the head of the jib the end of the
halliard which hangs down from the forward side
of this block using a " sheet bend " (Fig. 24),

which is a safe and simple means of attachment. At this point, if not before, you need to secure the other end of the halliard within reach, otherwise it may wind round the mast or playfully unreeve itself from the block, in which case you will have to lower the mast to put the halliard back.

Next, if there is a wire rope forestay from the masthead to the stem or bumkin, and spring hanks along the luff of the jib, snap the latter on to the stay, beginning with the top hank, and being careful to see that they are all snapped on in their right order down to the tack. Then attach the sheets to the jib clew, making certain that they are secure, because jib sheets are peculiarly liable to come adrift when the sail flogs, as it will if you are slow about sheeting it in.

In all probability you will find the main halliard has been left made fast to the yard, so just see that it is secure. The mainsheet, too, is probably ready rove through the block on the boom ; but you may find that the end of the sheet which is furnished with an eyesplice and thimble has been left loose, and wants shackling to the " mainsheet horse " (the horizontal metal rod which stands above the transom). Coil the free part of the mainsheet— the " fall "—on the stern seat to save trampling and tangling it.

The steel centreboard—sometimes termed the " plate "—may in this boat be too heavy for raising conveniently with a handle. If so, it will be lifted with a rope and two blocks, forming a " tackle " with a two-to-one purchase. There will in any event be a securing pin right through the top of the centreboard and its case to take the weight of the centreboard off the tackle when the boat is not being sailed.

To lower the centreboard before making sail, you will want first to take its weight off the pin by hauling on the tackle. Having withdrawn the pin, ease out the tackle again as far as it will run. But before finally making the rope fast on its cleat, which you will find on the centreboard case, pull in a few inches of rope. This will prevent the forward edge of the steel plate from straining the keel should you have the ill luck to strike the ground in such a way as to force the centreboard forwards.

After lowering the centreboard, pass the after end of the tiller under the mainsheet horse, and push it firmly into the slot in the rudder-head.

All the gear is now ready for you to make sail and to slip the chain, rope and buoy of the mooring overboard ; but before doing so, take stock of the conditions under which you are going to manoeuvre out of the anchorage. Other craft may lie in your way. The wind may be fluky and variable, and probably there is a current to allow for. This latter will greatly affect the boat's course before she has gathered speed ; so if the current is strong and there are other boats moored astern of yours you may need to get your boat forging ahead almost as soon as you have dropped the mooring.

Another possible difficulty, not encountered before

when you started out from a pontoon, is that of getting up the mainsail if the current should be holding the boat in a stern-to-wind position. At the pontoon you were able to turn the boat round to face the wind before casting her free. On a mooring that cannot be done, and with the wind from aft it would be a most awkward job to set the mainsail. What then is to be done ? The answer is : hoist the jib, and sail away under that alone. When clear of other craft you will be able to round up into the wind and set the mainsail. In a boat without a jib you would half hoist the mainsail to clear the anchorage, and fully set it as soon after as you could.

The above particularly awkward combination of circumstances has been cited simply to illustrate the fact that the thorniest of these problems has its solution. For the present we will assume that you are not confronted by a current opposed to the wind, and so can set the mainsail before letting go of the mooring.

In this case slack off the mainsheet, so that the boom will be free to swing, and heave away on the main halliard till the yard is right up, and the luff of the sail is stiff and straight. Make fast the halliard and if there is a lace holding the luff to the mast, take in any slack of this cord, and tie it in a small, neat coil to the large thimble or eyelet in the lower forward corner of the sail—the tack. After that, unless it is on a roller, hoist the jib. Both its sheets should be fast to cleats, but they should also be moderately slacked off so that the sail holds no wind, yet cannot flog about.

Should the jib be furled on a roller, all you need do to set this sail is to haul on one of its sheets while paying out the reel line.   See that this line winds snugly on to the reel, and make the free end fast, leaving no slack cord.   Should this reefing line be left at all loose it will become looped round the swivel below the reel, giving a lot of trouble.

Fig. 25.   Tubular Jam Cleat for jib sheets.

If, as is usually the way, the mooring chain is led on board to starboard of the stemhead, it will be easiest to sail away on the starboard tack, the boat heading away to port and leaving the mooring clear to starboard.   If you went away on the port tack the mooring buoy and its rope would be under the boat and likely to foul the centreboard or the rudder.

Should there be some other boat moored on your port side, forcing you to head away to your starboard hand, you will find it safest to free your riding chain and pass it, together with its buoy and rope, right round, outside your boat's stem to her port side. This will enable you to start off on the port tack, that is—heading away to starboard. By so doing you will leave both the mooring buoy and the other boat well out of your way on your port side.

Whether you let go of your mooring from over one bow or the other, it is an operation demanding care if the buoy is not to foul your boat or its own rope. First let the riding chain drop overboard; then pay out the rope hand over hand till you have only the buoy. Of this you should only let go when the tightening of the rope shows that you have drifted clear of the mooring, and will not sail over it.

Once safely away from the mooring, haul in and make fast the leeward one of the pair of jib sheets. Then haul in the mainsheet, and pull the tiller to windward, as you did when starting out in the lugsail dinghy.

In trimming the sheet—always the leeward one—of a jib care must be taken to see that the foot of the sail is adjusted at the same angle to the wind as is the foot of the mainsail; otherwise the wind will not flow smoothly between the two sails. The windward sheet must under all normal conditions of sailing be left quite slack, or it will cause a bagginess near the sail's clew. This sheet is only pulled in for the purpose of reducing the boat's speed by " backing " the sail to press the boat sternward.

As long as you are sailing a straight course it is unnecessary to alter the trim of the jib sheet ; but in tacking, as soon as you have pushed down the tiller to leeward, you should ease out the leeward jib sheet. This makes it easier for the boat to turn head to wind. As the boat turns away on to the new tack let the eased-out sheet run free, and immediately haul in and belay to its cleat the other sheet, which in its turn has now become the leeward one.

Of course, if you are alone, you will have to let go of the tiller to adjust the jib sheets. For this reason the cleats to which jib sheets are belayed should be located in the after part of the boat, so that you can control the tiller by leaning against it while tending these sheets.

In this boat, as in the lugsail dinghy, you will have to ease out the mainsheet to relieve the mainsail in hard puffs of wind ; but unless a really stiff squall strikes the boat, it will not be necessary to ease the jib sheet. Should you be compelled to do so because the boat is hard pressed, only slack off the sheet by an inch or two, or the sail will slat violently, and the sheet may tear off or break.

Apart from those that are fitted with wooden rollers, few small boats' headsails have any reefing tackle, and therefore they can only be set in moderate winds. In any case, whether the jib can be reefed or not, if you find you are carrying a little too much sail, make the first reduction by reefing the mainsail, tying down the first row of reef points, or with a roller boom, turning the latter round twice, so as to dispose of a strip of the mainsail about a foot deep. It is only when you find it necessary to tie down a second reef in the mainsail, or roll away a second foot of cloth round its boom if it reefs that way, that it is advisable to lower and stow the jib. Were you to lower the jib, yet keep the mainsail set without considerably reducing its area, the boat would persistently head into the wind like a weathercock, and even pulling the tiller hard to windward would probably not suffice to prevent her from doing so. After the mainsail has been twice reefed a roller jib may be slightly reduced in area, provided that this does not cause the boat to pull round head to wind violently, against the action of the rudder.

Already it has been mentioned that a boat's speed can be reduced by hauling in the windward jib sheet, and occasionally this is useful when picking up a mooring buoy, or avoiding some craft that is crossing your bows. If after hauling in the windward jib-sheet you slack the mainsheet well off, the boat will lie still except for drifting slowly sideways. In this condition she is said to be " hove-to." Since the tiller rarely needs touching to keep a boat lying still in this way, heaving-to enables one to deal with any small job needing both hands for a few minutes.

Small centreboard boats will not, like racing yachts, sail to windward under a headsail alone ; but a jib will by itself propel the boat at reduced speed with the wind over the stern or quarter.

The only conditions under which a jib, as ordinarily fitted, is ineffective, are those of sailing dead before the wind with the mainsail set as well. Then the latter starves the jib of wind, or " blankets " it.

Matters are improved if you have some means of " booming out " the jib over the side of the boat away from the mainsail, so that she runs " goose-winged " (a sail on each side). A handy makeshift method consists in fixing a small loop of cord to the clew of the jib to take an oar handle. The oar has to be lashed to the rowlocks or thwarts to keep it in position. Some " half-decked " boats (decked forward of the mast) carry a short boom, goose-necked to the forward side of the mast, and arranged to boom out the jib on either side of the boat as required. This, however, is not a popular arrangement, as three " guy " lines with fairleads and cleats are involved in controlling the boom.

In general, sailing a boat with a mainsail and headsail differs so little from the handling of a lug-rigged dinghy that we need not consider the trimming of the mainsheet or the tiller control in detail. On the other hand, since a start was made from a mooring the finish will be there, and something must be said about approaching a mooring buoy under various combinations of wind and tidal conditions.

At high water or low water, when there is no

current to complicate matters, one should first get to leeward of the buoy, and then beat up to it, preferably on the starboard tack to bring the buoy on that side over the windward bow. Steer as if to pass some six to eight feet to leeward of the buoy, and just before you come abreast of it push down the tiller to leeward. Then, if you have judged the distance and your boat's speed aright, she will swing round head to wind and stop with the buoy just under the starboard bow, where you can lift it on board.

Probably, you will miss the buoy the first time, either shooting the boat right past it, or turning too soon, so that the buoy is not reached before the boat stops dead and begins to drift down wind. In either case, pull in the windward jib sheet for a moment till the boat's head " pays off " (turns slightly away from the wind), then leave go of it, and haul in and belay the leeward jib sheet. You can then gather in the mainsheet, and beat up towards the buoy, hoping for better luck this time.

The approach to a mooring when there is a current to reckon with is made as it is in still water, provided that the current and the wind are not opposed. The only difference lies in the obvious fact that the boat will be carried backwards or sideways away from the buoy almost as soon as she loses headway. So wait till you are within two or three feet of the buoy before pushing down the tiller and luffing, or you will not reach it.

In both the above cases of approaching up-wind a jib, unless of the roller-reefing type, which can be instantly furled, is often a nuisance, flapping and flogging at your head as you reach for the buoy. If the boat has been found by experiment to handle satisfactorily under the mainsail alone, you may find it worth while to lower the headsail before coming into the anchorage. This may save a tussle with the sail at the crucial moment when you are stretching over the bow to get hold of the buoy.

It is when approaching your mooring with the wind and tide in opposition that you will reap one of the outstanding advantages of a sail set before the mast.

In this case it is necessary, as before, to meet the current bows-on, but the wind being from aft, you can only sail slowly enough to pick up the buoy if the mainsail has already been lowered, leaving the jib to carry the boat slowly forward over the current. Unless the wind is very strong this sail need not be lowered or furled till the buoy is safely on board.

In a boat without a headsail it is usually necessary, if the wind and current are opposed, to half lower the mainsail before approaching the buoy, and to haul the sail right down at the moment the buoy is reached.

This, it need hardly be said, complicates matters considerably. The half-lowered sail is much in one's way, and may refuse to come down at the critical moment, being filled with wind. A beginner will do best to stow his canvas while still clear of the anchorage, and row to the mooring—this cautious procedure is a good deal wiser than risking an embarrassed and spectacular finish !

CHAPTER VII

VARIOUS RIGS

So far it is only the lug and gunter types of mainsail that have received attention, because they are the most popular sails for small general purpose boats. Gunter sails cut long in the luff in proportion to the head on the yard are sometimes fitted in racing dinghies ; but as a racing dinghy's mainsail the Bermudian type is almost universal, and even for knock-about boats it is a strong rival to lugs and gunter sails.

The Bermudian sail has neither yard nor gaff, but is "jib headed," i.e., a purely triangular sail hoisted directly to the masthead. Along the luff it measures twice to two and a half times the length of its foot. Though called " Bermudian," the tall, narrow jib-headed type of mainsail has been used in many parts of the world and for hundreds of years ; but the word " Bermudian " has " stuck," and serves as well as would any other.

Although there is a general similarity between all Bermudian sails, there are many ways of arranging rigging to support their masts. The latter are inevitably very tall and slender, yet they must be kept straight if these sails are to set efficiently.

Much ingenuity has been expended in devising systems of wire staying for this purpose.

In very small boats, such as dinghies less than 12 ft. long, any system of wire rigging is very much in the way, and a disproportionately stout mast without rigging is usually preferred ; but in all larger craft the straightness of the mast is dependent on carefully devised and tensioned wire rigging, and we shall be dealing with this and other necessary " gadgets " in some detail.

Nearly all Bermudian masts are built up with a hollow centre so as to save weight, and this makes them somewhat expensive. With a purely knock-about rig, small for the size of the boat, one can make do with a solid mast. But a tall racing rig must be carried by as light a mast as possible, or the boat will be rendered " tender " (readily inclined to heel) by the excessive weight aloft.

In racing craft, with the mast weight cut very fine, the stresses set up by the sails have to be met by carefully disposed wire rigging. The wire used for dinghies and other small boats is either single-strand piano wire or the six stranded variety used in deep-sea sounding machines.

Boats of less than 16 ft. length have usually one pair of shrouds attached to the mast at the same height as the foresail halliard. These may be set out by a pair of " spreaders," which add to the supporting power of the shrouds, particularly if the boat is narrow at the gunwale. In addition to these lower shrouds there is often a pair of upper ones,

also with spreaders.   These upper shrouds may lead
right down to the gunwales, or they may be " dia-
mond shrouds," finishing on the
mast at the lower spreaders. (Fig.
26.)

With all Bermudian sails a forestay is necessary to prevent the
upper part of the mast from
bending aft. If it did that, the
leach of the Bermudian sail would
hang in slack folds, contributing
no driving force. The lower end
of the forestay is attached to the
boat's stemhead, and the upper
end to the mast between its top
and the foresail halliard block.
There may also be an upper
forestay to the masthead, in which
case the lower forestay will be
attached just above the foresail
halliard.

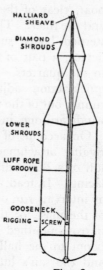

Fig. 26.

Between them, the shrouds and forestay or stays
are sufficient to counteract the strains on the mast
set up by a Bermudian sail ; but they do nothing to
prevent the mast from bending forwards, and if it
does that the luff of the foresail will go slack, and
render that sail incapable of being set sufficiently for
sailing to windward.

To keep the luff of the foresail taut and straight
the upper part of the mast must be pulled backwards
as far as the forestay admits, either by a single

backstay or by a pair of " runners." Of these two devices a backstay is preferable if it can be utilised. It extends from the masthead to the stern of the boat, clear of the end of the boom, the mainsheet and the tiller. This is not possible in short, transom-sterned boats, such as dinghies. The alternative device, a pair of runners, leads from the masthead to the quarters. Each runner has a lever or other quick-action adjustment for slacking off the lee runner out of the way of the boom, or tightening the windward one, in a matter of seconds.

On account of the mast being encumbered with rigging attachments it is not possible to hold the luff of a Bermudian sail to it with mast hoops or a lacing. Instead, metal slides attached to the luff at intervals run on a track screwed to the after side of the mast, or the latter is provided with a deep, narrow-mouthed groove from a little above the boom to the halliard sheave below the masthead, and the sail's luff rope is threaded into this. In up-to-date boats a similar groove in the boom is provided to hold the rope along the foot of the sail.

Of these two methods of sail attachment, that embodying a groove in the spar is preferable to the employment of a metal track in the case of boats and small yachts, because in small sizes the metal track is fragile, and if bent or nicked in the slightest degree it jams the slides, which are also liable to stick if the screws holding the track to the spar should be drawn loose so that their heads project. (Fig. 27.). Provided that both the mast and the

boom carry a track or groove, this class of attachment makes it possible to bend the sail to its spars
in a few minutes, and to keep it stowed in a bag
when out of use.   This lengthens the life of the sail
in comparison with one permanently bent to the
boom, and only protected by a sail cover.

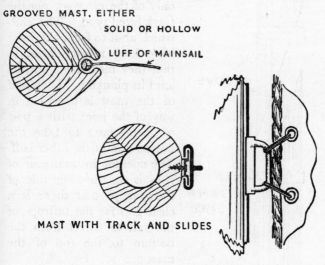

Fig. 27. Bermudian Sail Attachments.

Owing to its length being greater than that of the
boat, one cannot unship a Bermudian mast and stow
it on board if it is in one piece without a joint.   On
the other hand, dinghies at their moorings have
been capsized simply through the windage and
weight of their masts with no sail set.   To surmount

this disadvantage dinghies' masts, when they are of the solid type, are sometimes made of two pieces of equal length that can be readily joined together or separated for stowage.

These jointed masts are only of the grooved, not the track fitted type. The ends which abut to form the joint have long mitred faces, so that they meet like a scarfed joint in planking. Each half of the mast is provided in way of the joint with a pair of metal jaws to take the mitred end of the other half. The opening in each pair of jaws is on the after side of the spar, so that there is a clear gap for the luffrope of the sail to travel from the bottom to the top of the mast groove. (Fig. 28.)

As a further consequence of the tallness of Bermudian sails their luffs stretch and shrink very much with drying and wetting, and were ordinary fibre rope halliards used this trouble would increase to twofold owing to the stretching and shrink-

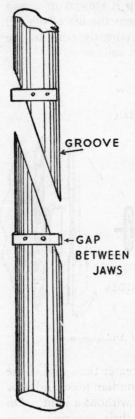

GROOVE

←GAP BETWEEN JAWS

Fig. 28. A jointed mast.

age of the rope. For this reason wire halliards are universal, a rope " tail " being spliced or shackled on to the free end of the wire to form a " hauling part." To enable the stretching of the sail to be taken up without touching the halliard, some boats have the boom gooseneck travelling on a short slide fitted to the mast. The weight of the boom then tightens the luff automatically. If the boom's weight is insufficient it can be bowsed down with a tack rope more easily than the sail could be hardened up with the halliard.

Not only must the luff of the sail be kept taut, the leach must be at least firm or it will droop into folds. The sails of medium-sized yachts have tightening cords from the headboard at the peak of the sail extending a few feet down the leach, the cord being adjustable in tightness. This is unusual in small Bermudian sails ; but they are practically always fitted with two or three " battens " (thin wooden or plastic laths) in pockets sewn to the after part of the sail and running perpendicularly to the leach. These battens are usually equally spaced between the head and the clew of the sail, and the middle one should be longer than the others, if there are three or more of them, to prevent a crease forming in the sail along the line of their forward ends.

When the sail is stowed, the battens should be removed from their pockets, otherwise they gradually strain the sail out of shape.

Like other boomed sails, Bermudians can be

D

reefed by roller gear or by reef points. Racing sails usually are provided with two or three rows of eyelets in place of points, so that a lace line can be threaded through from eyelet to eyelet with a turn round the boom between, using a single line from end to end. Threading the lace and drawing it tight is slow work, but the result is a snug reef.

Before the vogue of the Bermudian sail nearly all yachts and the larger private boats carried gaff mainsails. A gaff is like a gunter yard, but rarely more than half as long, and instead of standing vertically behind the mast it is slung at an angle of about 30 degrees by means of two separate halliards. As far as open boats are concerned this sail is obsolete, so we need not deal with it in detail. The same is true of the once very popular spritsail, which is now only used in Thames and Medway barges. This sail is practically oblong, with its luff laced to a rather short mast, and its peak extended by a spar called a " sprit " or " spreet," having its heel hooked to the mast a little above the level of the gunwale. The sprit leans aft from behind the mast much like the jib of a crane. It is kept standing, whether the sail is set or not, and the sail itself, instead of being lowered for stowing, is bunched in along the mast by a rope called a " brail." The worst feature of this rig is the permanently upstanding and only partially controllable sprit, which, to be stiff enough, must be a stout and therefore heavy spar. The spritsail which, but rarely carries a boom, is difficult to set flat enough for sailing close by the wind.

Up to this point, wherever a lugsail has been mentioned, we have referred to the standing lug ; because at the present time this particular variety of lugsail is the usual one in small pleasure boats.

There are, however, three other less common types of lugsail, which are worthy of mention, because each possesses some particular advantage, and possibly the reader might wish someday to give one or other of them a trial.

The three sails in question are the " dipping," " balance " and Chinese forms of lugsail, all three having this in common : at least one quarter of the sail's total area lies forward of the mast, thereby displacing the jib which is usually to be seen with a standing lugsail.

Nobody old enough to remember the Cornish and Scotch luggers of pre-motor days can look back on those picturesque fishing boats without a pang of regret at their disappearance. On the foremast they carried a great tanned dipping lugsail. Under the lifting influence of that sail, rather than plough the waves, they appeared to skim across the crests like seafowl.

The unquestionably high efficiency of this sail is due in no small measure to its standing well away from the mast, and so from the wind eddies surrounding it. The dipping lugsail is always set to leeward of the mast, with its tack hooked to an eye-plate on the windward gunwale (Fig. 29). This makes it necessary for the sail to be half lowered, and the forward end of the yard to be dipped round the after side of the mast when changing tack. The tack of the sail has at the same time to be unhooked, passed behind the mast, and re-hooked on the other gunwale. Needless to say, this can be an awkward task even for a large and experienced crew : so the dipping lugsail is unsuitable for narrow waters or for handling by amateurs. None the less, it gives a boat a wonderful speed and liveliness, as the reader will see for himself should he ever visit

Fig. 29. A dipping lug.

those remote north-western fringes of the British Isles where the dipping lug is still employed.

Very similar in shape to the dipping lug is the

balance lugsail. The outstanding difference lies in
the foot of the latter being laced to a boom, the
dipping lug never having one. It is this boom
which makes the character of the sail and its handling
completely different to those of the dipping lug.
The tack rope of the balance lug is fast to the boom
just forward of the mast, and heaving it down
flattens the whole sail, keeping it close against the
mast. There is no need to dip the yard or pass
the sail round the mast on tacking, and the flatness
of the sail makes it efficient when close-hauled to a
fine angle with the wind. On the other hand,
this sail suffers a loss of efficiency from the mast's
wind eddies, and it has none of the lifting power of
the dipping sail. The balance lug was formerly
used a great deal on the Norfolk Broads, and it is
generally considered rather a river sail than one
suited to sea boats. Under the usual river conditions of calm water and light winds this sail is only
surpassed by the Bermudian, which being taller, is
less liable to be screened from the wind by bushes
and high river banks. In open and therefore
disturbed waters the balance lug is far from being
a safe sail ; because the after end of the boom,
being unable to lift, may catch a wave crest, and
pin down the boat on her beam-ends. If that
happens, a capsize is inevitable.

While the balance lug has some claim to consideration as the best of the lugsail family for
sheltered sailing conditions, the Chinese lug has
many points in its favour for open waters, though

its virtues are not recognised in this country at the present time.

This sail, like the balance lug, carries a boom, and presents a considerable proportion of its area forward of the mast. Its outstanding feature is a series of battens running right across the sail from luff to leach. These battens make the sail somewhat heavy and stiff, so it does not fall into an efficient bird's-wing flow in a light breeze ; but it is exceptionally controllable in a hard wind, and can be reefed in a matter of seconds merely by easing the halliard. For this reason it has found favour in the past as the best sail for cruising canoes, " canoe yachts " and other small boats of limited stability.

Nowadays the Bermudian has replaced the Chinese lug even in canoes ; but the latter has certain virtues all its own, and it is therefore worth dealing with in detail.

The proportions of the Chinese lug (Fig. 30) are slightly different from those of the balance lugsail. It is taller for its width, and the yard is considerably shorter. The luff and the leach are both rounded out to an extent that is only possible on account of the battens.

The original junk sail, from which our European version has been derived, has battens of bamboo lashed across the sail on the side of it next the mast. Following the common practice in regard to yacht and boat sails, the battens of the Europeanised Chinese lug are housed in tubular pockets sewn to

the sail, though in some cases battens have been
fitted in pairs with the sail between, each pair
being held together at intervals with twine bindings
passed through eyelets in the sail.

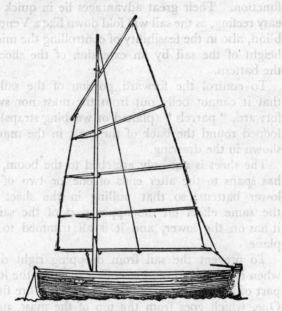

Fig. 30. A Chinese Lugsail.

The battens in any case have to be very supple
so that the sail may flex to the necessary bird's wing
curvature. For a dinghy's sail, single battens
should not be thicker than $\frac{1}{4}$ in., reduced to $\frac{3}{16}$ in.
just abaft the mast. Their width may be about

1¾ ins. Paired battens have, of course, to be thinner still.

The purpose of the battens is not merely to spread out the luff and leach of the sail. That is a minor function. Their great advantages lie in quick and easy reefing, as the sail will fold down like a Venetian blind, also in the feasibility of controlling the middle height of the sail by an extension of the sheet to the battens.

To control the forward portion of the sail, so that it cannot belly out from the mast nor swing forward, " parrels " (plaited or webbing straps) are looped round the back of the mast in the manner shown in the drawing.

The sheet is not only attached to the boom, but has spans to the after ends of one or two of the lower battens, so that pulling in the sheet has the same effect on the upper part of the sail as it has on the lower, and it is all trimmed to one plane.

To prevent the sail from dropping right down when it is lowered, and to collect together the lower part of it when a reef is taken in, " lifts " are fitted. One, which goes from the top of the mast, under the middle of the boom, and back again to the masthead, collects most of the sail : but to catch the forward part a second lift from the mast top may pass vertically down the sail on the side remote from the mast, go under the boom, and finish up attached to the mast a foot or so above the boom. This may sound rather complicated gear ; but the lifts never have to be adjusted, and they collect in the sail so neatly when a portion of it is reefed that, though reef points may be tied to make all snug and secure, their use is not essential.

CHAPTER VIII

SELECTING AND BUYING A BOAT

THE defects present in most hireable boats and their
gear are so irritating and troublesome that the
beginner in sail is certain, after his first season, to
wish very much for a boat of his own—one with a
tight hull and sound gear, a craft to be proud of.

If a general purposes boat is desired for sailing,
fishing, and bathing combined, it will be best to
buy her " off the stocks," that is to say: as a new
boat of the standardized type, with a standing
lugsail and galvanized centreboard.

At the present time, new 12 ft. sailing dinghies
of the utility class cost from £100 to £150; but a
used boat in good condition should be obtainable
for £50 if you study the " small advts " in the
yachting press.

Should the beginner have racing ambitions, there
are reasons why his first boat should be bought
second-hand. Racing dinghies cost nearly twice as
much as their utility counterparts, and are of delicate
construction. The beginner cannot, in any case,
expect to win races in his first season, except in
competition with other learners; so it would be a
pity to go to the cost of a new racing dinghy, and
possibly spoil her, before the owner is sufficiently
accomplished to do justice to such a craft.

The dinghies that are used for racing vary considerably in hull type. There are out-and-out " racing machines," such as the " International 14 footers " ; there are dinghies intermediately between these and pure utility craft, notably the " National 12 ft. dinghies " ; and there are various one-design classes, differing little from utility dinghies, that are organised by yacht and sailing clubs, mainly for the benefit of their junior members.

As the name implies, " one-design " boats of any particular class are all alike, and so give close racing between themselves. They do not often pass into the hands of purchasers other than members of the club sponsoring the class ; and that is one of the reasons why the beginner should seek club membership.

Yacht and sailing clubs vary considerably in organisation, outlook, and advantages offered the individual member. An exclusive club of high repute lends prestige to its membership. But even in the unlikely event of his election, a beginner will reap very little benefit ; and he will be much more at home in one of those small sailing clubs where there is little money in evidence, but a great deal of enthusiasm. Membership of such a club is usually granted after an interview with the club secretary, who will also assign a locker for gear, a mooring and other individual facilities on payment of the annual subscription.

Apart from these certain benefits, the club secretary is a likely person to know of a good boat that may be for sale locally, and he would certainly be willing to pass unbiased judgment on any boat that the beginner might already contemplate purchasing.

As a prelude to buying a boat it is advisable to look over as many as possible, both new and second-hand, before even beginning to come to a decision. Used boats are offered at prices quite at variance with their actual values, which are not easy to assess.   Would-be sellers usually ask more than they expect to get, and the price has to be beaten down stage by stage to a figure the buyer considers reasonable.

Many a " tore out " " as ripe as a pear " is palmed off on some inexperienced enthusiast merely through being freshly painted.   All thickly painted dinghies should be regarded with suspicion ; because small boats when new are varnished, and they are very rarely painted before paint becomes necessary to fill in and conceal defects.   Provided a dinghy is varnished, anyone looking carefully can see if her planks are split or her ribs cracked.   A split that will close when the boat has been a few hours in the water is not a very serious defect in itself : but it does matter if in the region where the split occurs the ribs are also broken, for then the split may run right down the plank, necessitating a new one.

Buying a boat the damaged planks of which have been cobbled with " tingles " (patches) is just as unwise as accepting a craft with open rents left for the purchaser to make-good. Mere patching is not only unsightly. It is unreliable, and the only satisfactory method of dealing with a damaged plank is to replace the whole, or a considerable length of it, with new timber. This is delicate work, particularly in a clench-built boat, and consequently expensive.

Apart from wide splits in the planking, which commonly occur in the sharp curve of the bilge, a serious source of leakage frequently found in sailing dinghies is a strained centreboard case. Usually this has been caused by the centreboard striking a hard bottom and putting a severe lateral strain on the hull. The joint between the centreboard case and the keel is thereby opened, and the only cure is to take the case out and re-seat it. That is work for a boatbuilder, and must be allowed for in the price. Such a leak you will not discover till the boat is afloat, and on that account the intending purchaser should never clinch his bargain without a trial trip.

Not only will taking the boat for a short trial sail disclose any serious hull defects ; it will show the quality and condition of the sailing gear. A mere inspection of the sail or sails will give some idea of their age ; but it will not show whether they set fairly, or have been stretched out of shape by careless handling. An old sail that sets in a fair curve is preferable to a new one that has been pulled into permanent bags and wrinkles.

Unquestionably, it is advisable to start boat owner-

ship with a second-hand craft. But owing to the demand for used boats far exceeding the supply, this is
quite likely to prove impossible, and a new boat from
stock or built-to-order will have to be obtained.
Naturally, this involves a higher price ; but if the
new boat is built to order you have a say in the
choice of materials, and should obtain a boat
that thoroughly meets your requirements.

As instances of timber appropriate to particular
conditions of service, it may be said that if the boat
is entirely for river use, and you do not mind the
extra cost, cedar is a beautiful wood for the planking.
It is also of light weight, and amply strong for a
boat sailing inland waters. For sea use tougher
wood is necessary. First class construction for small
sea boats calls for silver spruce topsides, and wych
elm bottom planking. This latter timber is the best
obtainable in its resistance to abrasion.

Cheaper than silver spruce, and almost as good,
is Scotch larch. Oregon and Columbian pine are
both cheaper still, but to be avoided, as they lack
durability.

Boats built to a high specification have transoms
of teak or mahogany : but common English elm,
which is cheap, is perfectly satisfactory for a sea
boat, though it will not last in river water.

The backbone of a dinghy, consisting of her keel,
stem and sternpost, should be of straw-coloured
British oak with the grain running down the whole
length of the timber. Make sure about this last
point, because in some poorly built boats nearly

straight grained timber is used for curved portions, such as the stem. A piece of wood like that will split diagonally across its length sooner or later. For ribs there is only one satisfactory timber, namely Canadian rock elm, which is close grained and pale in colour, rather like split cane. For this, oak and ash are cheap substitutes; but oak ribs break where they are sharply bent, and ash ones are liable to early decay. The " knees " (brackets) should be of oak with the grain curving round from tip to tip. Another satisfactory wood for knees is apple wood, very tough and almost white. It is used in West Country boatbuilding for knees and breasthooks.

It may be taken almost for granted that any dinghy the reader may buy will have clenched-laid planking, which is much more common than the carvel build with flush-fitted planking. On a cost basis the former is best, for it gives lightness and strength at moderate cost. Purely for the extra speed obtainable from a smooth bottom and bilges a high grade carvel dinghy with almost invisible seams, and ribs but 2 ins. apart, is preferable to a clench-built boat.

On the other hand, a cheap carvel dinghy, with thick planking and widely spaced ribs, is heavier and weaker than a corresponding boat with clenched planking.

At the present time a quite differently constructed class of dinghy is achieving popularity, namely craft of " moulded " construction. These are built up from three or more layers of wood veneer cemented together with synthetic resin cement under light pressure. Some years ago boats of similar construction, but cemented with casein glue, appeared on the market. Owing to the perishable nature of casein glue these were not a success; but the resin cements are enormously strong and definitely waterproof, so these resin-bonded boats may be accepted with full confidence. In price they are reasonable; they are very light, and entirely smooth inside and out, also they are easy to mend.

The skin of these boats, being very thin, will not stand much abrasion; but this weakness can be met by fitting rubbing strips along the bottom.

Nothing has so far been said about the shape or "lines" of the boat a beginner should buy, because —particularly when purchasing second-hand—he will probably have to accept any boat of the desired size that is in good condition and reasonably priced. None the less, should there be a choice, the following points should be noted: stability and carrying power both depend on a broad flattish bottom, and a full-bodied boat will not prove excessively slow or heavy to row provided her bow and stern are well tucked up; that is to say, the bows should be sharp under water and wide above, while the transom is sufficiently raised to only just rest on the water when the boat is fully loaded. Fullness of hull, desirable as it is in a utility dinghy, which may have to carry considerable loads, or alternatively, keep her crew dry in rough water, detracts from speed, and so must not be a leading feature in a racing dinghy.

The bottom of a racing dinghy is vee'd rather than flat. She is also shallower and narrower than the utility class of boat. To save weight, her stern is very low, and her planking extra thin. Some remarkable open water passages have been made in racing dinghies; but essentially they are sheltered water craft, only to be nursed through an open sea passage by expert helmsmanship.

Whilst emphasis has been laid on the general superiority of dinghies as the class of boat best suited for elementary sail training, there are various other types of small boats presenting special advantages of their own, and of these the sharpie is a popular example. During the last decade the word " sharpie " has been stretched to cover all sorts of boats that have angular cross-sections; but strictly speaking the name is only applicable to keel-less boats presenting no angle along the centre-line of the bottom, which in cross-section is perfectly flat. They only have angles where the bottom is joined to the sides, and these angles form the " chines." They are slab-sided and slab-bottomed craft that can readily be built from resin-bonded plywood. (Fig. 31.) " flat-bottomed," however, does not describe them. To make them capable under sail they are given " rockered " bottoms, that is—bottoms bent upwards at bow and stern. Any truly flat-bottomed boat,

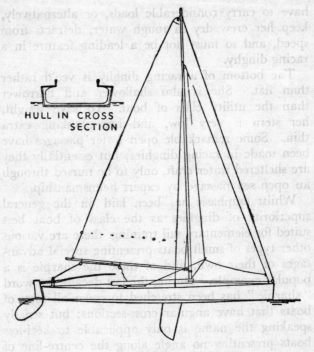

HULL IN CROSS
SECTION

Fig. 31. A Bermudian rigged sharpie.

such as a wildfowling punt, is extremely sluggish under sail or oars, and throws the slightest ripple right over herself.

Compared with dinghies, sharpies are narrow, shallow hulled, and much longer for the same carrying capacity. Mainly on account of their low sides they are always decked, with a narrow cockpit.

When sailing, the crew always sit on the deck. Their feet are below the leeward side-deck of the cockpit, and with this purchase they can safely lean out to windward to balance the boat. This leaning out, or " hiking," is essential with any weight in the wind, as sharpies are " tender " (lack stability), and capsizing is more likely than with a dinghy. However, an upset matters less—at least in calm water— because the cockpit is made so narrow that its lower coaming is above water-level even when the boat is right on her side with her mast touching the water. With the boat in that condition, the crew have only to collect in the sails to be able by hiking to bring their craft upright again.

The sharpie's weakness for capsizing suddenly certainly renders her at best a second choice for the beginner. She throws up a lot of spray, and any real waves knock the speed right out of her. On the other hand, she makes a very good inland water craft, with—unlike the dinghy—dry stowage for camping kit. In small sharpies, measuring 14 ft. or less in length, sleeping aboard is hardly possible unless the usual centreboard is replaced by a pair of lee-boards, as the centreboard case takes up the best of the room under the deck.

A 16 ft. sharpie should afford rather cramped sleeping quarters for two, if an awning is suspended from the boom over the cockpit. So easy are sharpies to build that by far the greater number are amateur productions.

The rig most in favour for sharpies is that of the

Bermudian sloop, with roller reefing to both jib and mainsail. A sharpie will only carry three-quarters of the sail area customary for a dinghy of the same length ; but of the two she is the smaller boat in other dimensions, and so requires less sail to drive her.

CHAPTER IX

THE CARE OF HULL AND GEAR

To any keen boat owner there is always satisfaction
in discovering improvements that might be made to
his craft, and in executing them in leisure moments,
particularly during the winter months. It is
possible to leave all such work to professional yacht
outfitters ; but to do so is to sacrifice one of the
pleasures of possessing a sailing boat.

The most delicate items of boat gear are always
the sails, and they repay one for constant and careful
attention. When in actual service, any light cotton
sail undergoes a great deal of stretching, which
strains the fabric, and tends to pull the sail out of
shape. This is unavoidable ; but it can be com-
pensated by leaving the sail slack in every direction
when it is not being used. It will then to a large
extent contract and recover itself.

Unless it has been treated with some reliable
preservative, no sail must ever be packed away in a
bag or a locker while it is the least bit damp, or it
will become rotten with mildew. In warm weather
this can happen in a matter of two or three days.
If a sail is damp, yet cannot be hung up to dry, leave
it in the open, even in the rain, rather than cover it

in an effort to prevent it from becoming wetter still. No harm will come from the wet, as long as the sail has perfectly free ventilation. Should it be necessary to leave a sail attached to its spars in an open boat for weeks together, provide a sail coat of Willesden canvas that can be arranged tent-fashion over the sail, using the spars as ridge pole. The " eaves," if one may so describe the lower edges of the coat, should be loosely laced together, leaving an air gap of several inches under the sail. A coat for a lugsail having a yard and boom say 10 ft. long should itself be 11 ft. long, to extend beyond the ends of the spars, and prevent rain drops running along them to the sail. Its width should be not less than 2 ft., so that it can hang down over the loosely bundled sail, which will have a fairly free air circulation without rain splashing on to it.

Since so much care has to be taken to protect sails from mildew, it may be wondered why so few of them are chemically preserved. The reasons are various. First, any preservative adds to the sail's weight, and most of them also stiffen the fabric. Then there is usually some uncertainty as to how long the protection will last, and finally, even the safest process may weaken the cotton cloth if unskilfully applied. The old fashioned fishermen's preservative methods—treatment with cutch fixed by bichromate of potash, or ochre painted on with oil—are inappropriate for thin, delicate boat sails. Unless they are to be passed for treatment to some knowledgeable firm of sailmakers, all that can safely be done is brushing on with a distemper brush an ounce of soft clean paraffin wax dissolved in a quart of best quality paraffin lamp oil. The latter will slowly evaporate, leaving a very thin film of wax that will for a time protect the cotton. The wax collects dirt, but can be washed out with hot water. This wax application, though only effective for one sailing season at most, can be repeated indefinitely, without the least risk to the sail.

Wax is also a good preservative for cordage; but to prevent it rubbing off it has to be put on mixed with lubricating oil. This, of course, is messy, and unsuitable for the gear of a smart dinghy. On the other hand, it is highly to be recommended for the hard worked gear of any boat used for sea fishing, when supple ropes that neither jam in the blocks nor harden with wet are far more important than mere appearances.

In spite of the fact that it shrinks and slackens according as it is wet or dry, sailcloth is stable in comparison with the small flax cord which is used for lacings and for lashing the corners of sails to yards and booms. Flax is particularly troublesome when new; so if possible employ cord that has had some use, or at least give it a good stretching before putting it into service.

The wire ropes used for shrouds, for forestays, and for the halliards of Bermudian sails are composed of fine plough steel wires galvanized and " laid up " (twisted) together. These ropes, though very thin, hardly stretch at all; but they present their own particular problem—that of rust prevention.

So long as the zinc coating is unbroken, rusting is not to be expected : but the zinc is bound to be rubbed off to some extent when the end of a wire is bent back and spliced into an eye by interweaving the wires : and there are these eye splices at both ends of all wire ropes. The usual protective covering of a wire eye splice is a " service " (binding) of fine cord, soaked in boiled linseed oil and then varnished. However, the extremely thin wire ropes used aboard small boats can be more effectually protected by warming and dipping their ends in boiled oil, and then, when the oil has dried, covering them with a tight wrapping of insulating tape. The result is not very neat, but it is highly effective.

All the trouble connected with wire eye splices can be avoided by the substitution of tubular steel yokes, as used with aeroplane wires. Into these the ends of the ropes are inserted and soldered.

Your boat's spars, although they are likely to outlast several suits of sails, need occasional examination. In particular the foot of the mast wants watching, because the step, into which it fits, may keep it wet and cause it to rot. The block of wood forming the mast step should have a hole right through it from side to side as a drain for the mortice.

With regard to the preservation of the boat herself, and of such items as the bottom boards and rudder, it should be borne in mind that however carefully these are kept varnished or painted, they will still absorb water and become heavy if immersed for more than a few hours at a time; and for this reason racing dinghies are kept ashore, and only put afloat just before taking part in a race.

The weight due to soakage naturally matters less in the case of a knockabout dinghy. Still, it is to be avoided if possible. Over-drying is as bad, if not worse than the waterlogging of a boat, because it shrinks the wood, and cracks the varnish at the seams, thereby setting up leaks. If a boat is left ashore, bottom up in hot sunshine, for a few days, her planking is quite likely to crack right through. Soaking the boat in water may close such cracks for the time being; but they will gradually become wider and ultimately necessitate repairs.

To decide whether old paint and varnish should be stripped right off before more is applied is not easy. In the case of paint, there is no absolute necessity to scrape the wood bare unless the old paint is coming off in flakes or powder; but it makes a boat noticeably heavy if she is painted three or four seasons running without considerable sandpapering in between to reduce the thickness of the old paint before adding more.

Varnishing is quite a different matter from painting. Varnish is not so protective, nor does it last as long as paint. On the other hand, and unlike paintwork, one can touch up thin spots in a varnished surface without producing a patchy appearance or having to wait days together for the new coat to harden.

Of paint and varnish removing preparations there are two distinct types, namely the old-fashioned alkali solutions, and the more recently introduced volatile " dopes " soluble in such vehicles as amyl alcohol. The former consist in the main of caustic soda in concentrated aqueous solution, and they are commonly referred to as " sougimougi." This caustic mixture, if applied two or three times in succession, with scraping between, will take off the hardest and thickest paint ; but, unfortunately, it penetrates the wood, and may seriously harm it, unless washed out with repeated hosing and scrubbing. It is also possible to avoid after-effects by neutralising the alkali that remains in the wood with a weak acid, such as white vinegar, but this is not entirely dependable.

The volatile paint and varnish removers entail less risk, but they are more expensive, and owing to their volatility one must keep on scraping continuously as the remover is applied or it will dry, leaving a hard crust, which calls for a further application before one can scrape it off.

In cases where it is desired to remove only an outer layer of varnish because the under coats appear to be firm and clear, a paste made up of soap shavings and washing soda, if left on for an hour or two, will soften the outer varnish so that it can be scrubbed off without denuding the wood.

Wash the exposed undercoat thoroughly, before re-varnishing it. This method does not render the wood light coloured " like new " ; but it results in its economical and effective protection.

There is one part of any centreboard boat that suffers greatly from neglect, because of its inaccessibility, and that is the inside of the centreboard case. Only during winter storage does this case dry out sufficiently for the wood to be painted, and then it is not uncommonly forgotten. The simplest method of treatment is, after removing the C.B., to wind flannel round a stick and use this as a brush to lay on either black varnish or red lead in linseed oil. To do the work more thoroughly, instead of brushing on the black varnish or paint, one should temporarily plug the slot in the keel below the case with wood and putty, and then fill the case right up to the top with whichever coating is preferred, leaving it there for a day or two before draining off the surplus. This is a troublesome and extravagant procedure, but effective.

If, when it is new, a galvanized steel centreboard is well greased, and so maintained by being coated annually, the zinc protection will last indefinitely. Without grease the zinc will wear thin after a season or two, and rusting will result. Nothing will absolutely stop this rusting, once started, except re-galvanizing ; but it can be retarded by washing off the salt, and black varnishing the C.B. when the boat is hauled out for the winter. This must not be delayed till the spring, as the salt on the apparently dry C.B. will be damp enough to go on eating into the steel during the winter months.

To prevent stones from entering it, the slot in the keel under the centreboard case may have a pair of rubber strips fitted. These become torn, and are likely to need replacing with new strips cut from the discarded inner tube of a car tyre.

The temptation, when putting a boat into winter storage, to leave all maintenance jobs till the spring re-fit, is strong, but it should be resisted for the following reasons : at the end of the summer one knows what repairs and renewals are required ; but by the following spring it is probable that some items will have been forgotten. Again, dirt left in a boat all winter may, if it is at all moist, form a breeding-ground for rot. So at least the hull should be cleaned out before storage.

Thoroughly cleaning a clench-built dinghy is a long, difficult job. A wash down with a hose and scrubber makes her look clean inside, but there may still be a whole bucketful of dirt stuck in the crevices where the ribs cross the plank landings. The average dinghy has about 500 of these narrow, wedge-shaped spaces, and every one of them needs raking out with a stiff, bent wire. The dirt so loosened is easiest to remove with a vacuum cleaner. But in default of that one must turn the boat upside-down on trestles, and tease the dirt out with a pot scourer or other narrow, stiff brush. Even then, there are so many niches where the dirt can re-settle that it is often a half-hour's job to get rid of the last of it. In most dinghies it is the ribs that show rot before anything else, and hidden dirt is invariably the cause.

Not uncommonly it is in the course of cleaning a boat out that the owner first becomes aware of cracks in their early stages of development. The planks most likely to crack are those at the turn of the bilge, midway between the keel and the gunwale. These planks when they are sawn out are given considerable " sny " (curvature of outline), and their grain rarely runs down them from end to end, so they are not very strong. Moreover, they have to be much bent and twisted into place on the hull. Hence they are not infrequently a source of trouble when a boat is subjected to severe strain.

There is no satisfactory way of closing a wide split in a boat's planking. A length of at least three feet has to be removed from the plank in way of the split, and a new length scarfed in by a competent boatbuilder.

Small cracks running down the centre of a plank, and not inclined to split its edges, are the only ones with which the owner should attempt to deal himself.

These should be covered on the outside with " tingles " (patches) not of wood as is commonly done, but of thin sheet copper, fitted and fixed in the following manner :

Scrape and sandpaper the wood all round the crack, both inside the boat and outside ; varnish these cleaned surfaces thickly, and when the varnish has become tacky cover the split on both sides with strips of thin calico 1½ ins. wide. Put on more varnish, cut a strip of thin, soft copper sheet 2 ins. wide and 4 ins. longer than the split, and with very fine copper tacks ¼ in. long, nail it over the split on the outside. The holes for the tacks will have to be made at ½ in. intervals with a bradawl, their line slightly staggered to avoid making a second split, and the edges of the copper should be pressed into the wood, so that nothing can catch in them. The copper should finally be painted to match the wood, and the calico strip inside the boat may be similarly painted. This inner strip serves to keep water and dirt out of the wood. It may want re-sticking at the annual overhaul.

CHAPTER X

CRUISING PREPARATIONS

To anyone unversed in open boat seamanship any coastwise passage in a sailing dinghy is bound to appear as a foolhardy escapade. For the beginner in sail it can be so ; but after a few short day trips in open waters the learner should be capable of nursing his craft through a moderate " lop " of sea, and of weighing up the degree of risk involved in any projected coastwise venture. It is safe to say that he will by then know enough about his own and his boat's limitations not to run blindfold into situations of positive danger.

The reason why no absolute novice should attempt coastwise cruising is that safety lies far more in the capabilities of the crew than in the qualities of their craft. A decked and ballasted sailing yacht, even of the smallest size, will sail herself untended for hours, and pick herself up unscathed after being laid on her beamends by a squall. That, unfortunately, is beyond the capacity of open boats, however large. They need careful steering under all conditions. If the wind suddenly strengthens or the wave crests begin to break, sail may have to be shortened in a hurry. The crew must therefore be both agile and cool-headed.

127

While expert boat sailors have demonstrated the possibility of making open water passages with racing dinghies even under adverse weather conditions, it is only utility-type boats of a good size that are really suitable. Racing dinghies have insufficient freeboard to keep the spray out ; they have not the carrying capacity for adequate camping kit ; and the quick, sensitive helmsmanship which they call for, puts too great a strain on one for a passage lasting all day and possibly into the hours of darkness.

High, buoyant ends and a full bilge are the points of design to look for ; the boat should be " all boat," well rounded out in every dimension. On the other hand, the construction has got to be on the light side or, even when she is stripped bare, the boat's weight will be too great for her crew to launch or beach her without assistance. The physical strength and weight of the crew must, of course, have considerable bearing on the question of boat dimensions ; but taking an average crew and kit weight, an 11 ft. boat with 4 ft. 6 ins. beam will suit the lone cruiser, whilst a crew of two will need at least 2 ft. more length and a beam of 4 ft. 8 ins. These linear dimensions may not suggest much difference in size between a one-man and a two-man boot ; but actually they imply a marked difference in carrying capacity.

Provided that it is simple and strong, the sailing gear of a cruising boat may be the same as is used in her for ordinary day sailing. The crew's health and comfort, on the other hand, depend on the very careful selection of the rest of the equipment, from the bottom boards and bailer to the blankets and cooking stove.

As will be appreciated, keeping one's bedding, spare clothes and food dry in rainy and boisterous weather is by no means easy, for not only is there the rain and spray from above, but the bilge water spurting up from below the floor boards. The ordinary bottom or " burthen " boards, with gaps between them, lying directly on the boat's bottom, are always wet on top so long as there is a quart of bilge water swilling about under them. That, of course, will not do. They must be raised on transverse battens of wood 1 in. deep, or—better still—they may be replaced by a close-boarded platform, level on top and extending over the middle third of the boat's bottom, that is to say : from a little aft of the mast to the after end of the centreboard case. It is in this central third of the boat that all the heavy, bulky kit items should be stowed, wrapped in canvas and wedged under the thwarts, so that they cannot possibly shift, however lively the boat's motion. Under or just forward of the stern seat it is essential to leave a gap in the floorboards large enough to serve as a bailing well. By shifting your weight aft you can make the bilge water collect there, whence it can be scooped overboard.

The ordinary British type of bailer, precisely like a scullery bowl, is an unsatisfactory article. It will not collect the last few pints of bilge water ; its

E

metal rim bruises the boat's timbers ; and if dropped overboard it sinks. The all-wood Scandinavian bailer, shaped like a shovel, has none of these bad characteristics. An even better bailer of the same shape can be made from such tough but pliant materials as shoe leather or canvas-lined sheet rubber. (Fig. 32.)

Many people object to the heaviness of ash oars ; but they are the least likely to break when you are

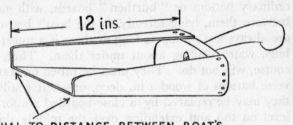

EQUAL TO DISTANCE BETWEEN BOAT'S
RIBS LESS HALF-INCH

Fig. 32. An effective bailer.

landing or launching your boat from a rocky shore, and that is a most important consideration, as, though a spare rowlock should be provided, there will not be room on board for an extra oar.

Some boat sailors may be attracted by the labour-saving charms of an outboard motor, and one of the very light type will earn its keep on a trip in semi-sheltered waters. On the other hand, all outboards are difficult to stow compactly, and none of them take kindly to a mixture of salt water and sand in the carburettor ; so if contemplating a trip that involves open beach landings, it is better that the outboard should be left at home.

Coir rope is commonly used with small boats' anchors, but it is bulky, picks up water and mud, and readily tangles. A hard, smooth rope, such as lightly tarred hemp, is much to be preferred. It should be of $1\frac{1}{2}$ ins. circumference. Carry as large a coil of this as can be accommodated below thwart-level forward of the mast.

Anchors are made in such a bewildering variety of forms—each claimed by the makers to be the best—that selecting one is difficult. Listen to all opinions, but take them with a grain of salt. Any anchor should prove trustworthy that draws a single sharp point into the seabed no matter how it lies on the bottom. Do not be persuaded into buying any anchor with two points or " palms " bearing on the seabed at once ; for neither point will obtain a grip, owing to the meagre weight of a small boat's anchor, which at the most will not exceed some 14 lb.

If it were certain that in cruising one would never be out of sight of land it would be unnecessary to provide a compass ; but anywhere on tidal waters visibility may suddenly be cut down to a dozen yards or less by fog, in which case one may turn circles or proceed in an entirely wrong direction through lack of a compass. This need not be an expensive instrument. Any pocket compass will do that has a needle the ends of which are clearly distinguishable as north-pointing and south-pointing.

Charts, sailing directories and tide tables would be useful to the cruising boat sailor could he accommodate them safely ; but it is very difficult to handle and preserve such articles in an open boat. Most charts are cumbersome and expensive, whereas folding pocket maps are comparatively cheap. The latter give most of the information likely to be required, and if a chart or sailing directory can be temporarily borrowed, the best course is to extract and pencil in on the map such notes regarding tides and seamarks as are likely to prove of service. This is particularly important with regard to the direction of tidal currents, for a dinghy is at their mercy. In many districts the tide changes its direction several hours before or after high and low water. An understanding of the tides enables one to reap the advantages offered by favourable currents. On the other hand, anyone without this essential knowledge is likely to spend much time and energy fruitlessly "bucking" currents that flow up to three miles an hour in the wrong direction.

As vulnerable as charts and much more expensive is the whole range of navigational instruments that are used for laying off courses on charts and finding a vessel's position. Fortunately, none of these are required, as one can make a near enough guess as to one's position and direction when the shore is the whole time in plain view and often at a stone's throw.

So small is the carrying capacity of a dinghy that camping and personal kit has to be cut down to bare essentials, and few people will agree as to what is absolutely necessary and what is not. Everybody will realise that one must have oilskins or a dependable waterproof coat ; but the number of cooking utensils and the quantity of bedding are matters about which differences of opinion are inevitable. As a standby, if not for everyday use, a Primus stove, with paraffin, methylated spirit and cleaning needles is highly advisable ; because one must not count on always being able to collect dry sticks and light a fire on the beach or river bank. Again, there is many an estuary or stretch of coast where for miles one will not come upon a source of drinkable water. So, unless sure of there being clear river water or piped house supplies, one will include in the kit either a clean petrol can or a stoneware jar of a capacity of 1 gallon per man. Naturally, there are cases calling for more than this, but one can make do on as little as a quart of water a day at a pinch, and the fact of having a few pints in hand relieves one's worst anxiety when the local water resources are an unknown quantity.

Some people take a light-weight tent for camping ashore, others prefer to sleep in the boat under an awning rigged over the boom supported by the mast. If such an awning is to be used it should be thoroughly tried out beforehand ; as it is not easy to rig one in such a way that it will stand up to wind and rain without letting in draughts and driblets of wet. At a pinch, one can empty the boat of all gear, turn her over, prop up the leeward side, and

sleep underneath. This hardly spells comfort, but
at least it assures one of shelter in the worst of
weather. In that respect yacht and boat cruising
like caravanning, has an advantage compared with
other methods of travelling. There are no worries
about bed and board, for you always have them with
you.

The selecting of food for a boat expedition is again
so much a matter of individual taste that only a
few general hints will be given here. Always take
advantage of fresh provisions when they can be
eaten before they " go off," because they are almost
always more wholesome, more palatable and cheaper
than preserved foods. On the other hand, fresh
meat and fish keep for only half a day in warm
weather if packed without ventilation in tins, so
one must carry at least a small stock of " iron
rations " together with dried or salted food, such as
bacon, cheese, kippers, and ham, in addition to
cereals. For those who like it, cheese is a wonderful
standby. In fact, helped out with apples and plain
biscuits, one could live on it comfortably.

Lever top tins and canisters are sufficiently waterproof for carrying sugar and condiments ; but tea
and ground coffee need absolutely air-tight con-
tainers. These and matches should be stored in
corked bottles.

Of whisky and other stimulants one has to beware.
Living this strenuous, simple life a man is more
affected by alcohol than under more civilised
conditions. However, a tot when turning in on a

chilly, damp night may not only be welcome but advisable. Spirits are " medical stores " to the boat cruiser, and a flask of whisky or rum should not be omitted.

CHAPTER X

ESTUARY CRUISING

At the beginning of the preceding chapter it was
pointed out that the technique and conditions that
apply to boat cruising differ from those of yachting.
A yacht is, or should be, a vessel capable of being
manoeuvred and controlled in winds as strong as
are likely in the summer months round the coasts
of England. Should a gale threaten, she will
usually be able to reach a harbour in time. If not,
she will heave to, and ride out the blow in deep
water. A well found and manned sea-going yacht
is in no danger of shipwreck, unless she is driven
backwards on to a lee shore, and that is an extremely
rare occurrence.

With open boats bad weather is a very different
matter. When sailing along the coast one must
always have at the back of one's mind the possibility
of having to beach one's craft or make a race of it
for harbour should the wind suddenly strengthen
and raise a sea that might presently become
dangerous for her. A wind that a sailor would
only class as a " strong breeze," if blowing contrary
to the direction of the tidal current will in less than
an hour churn up waves so steep that their crests
break heavily. With luck and skill an open boat

136

may be kept from swamping under such conditions
—or she may not. But the point, which cannot be
over-emphasized, is this : at the first hint of bad
weather an open boat must be got into shelter,
either ashore or in a harbour. Once the wind and
waves approach gale conditions it will no longer be
possible either to keep her afloat or beach her
through the rows of shore breakers.

It should be obvious, when these limitations have
been taken into consideration, that the best cruising
ground for a boat is not the open coast, but some
arm of the sea presenting sheltering land on one
side or the other according to the wind's direction,
also shingle bars or islands plentifully scattered
between the shores, so that a boat will never be
very far from a haven of refuge under the lee of such
features.

The coasts of Great Britain do not afford many
large landlocked areas of water of the type indicated.
The Solent in the South and the Firth of Clyde in
the north alone approach the ideal. But there are
a considerable number of river estuaries that are
reasonably safe for the boat sailor who has had some
experience ; while for the complete novice there
are the Norfolk Broads, where at least he will not
be put out of countenance, since most Broadlands
sailors are also beginners, learning the ropes in
hired cruisers.

For Londoners the nearest cruising ground is the
inner portion of the Thames Estuary west of a line
from Clacton in Essex to Whitstable in Kent.

These are muddy waters, and the shores are for the most part flat and uninspiring ; but it is a safer cruising ground than most, and one that will teach the beginner all he needs to learn about tidal currents and shoal water pilotage.

Just as coastal navigation in connection with a boat has to differ from the yachtsman's practice, so does estuary pilotage for the cruising boat contrast with that practised by the pilots of large vessels. The latter are concerned with keeping ships in the deep channels between the sandbanks ; whereas, owing to the very real danger of being run down by steamers, the boat sailor must acquaint himself

Fig. 33.   Going in, " Cans " to port and " Cones " to starboard.

with the lie of the ship channels in order to be able to avoid them. This danger from the steam traffic cannot be over-stressed. Only cross the busy steam lanes when they cannot be avoided, and do so by daylight.

Provided that visibility extends to a mile, the deep water channels are easily located, on account of the buoys marking the edges of the shoals on either hand. To a vessel entering a navigable channel from seaward the shoals on her starboard side are indicated by conical buoys, those to port by flat topped " can " buoys.   Spherical buoys, painted

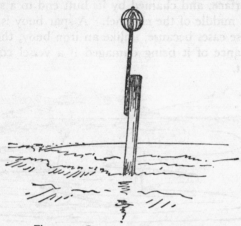

Fig. 34.   Beacon marking sandbank.

with stripes, mark the tips of shoals splitting a fair-way into two channels.   Large sandbanks that are uncovered at low tide are in some instances marked by beacons.   These are large posts topped with latticework identification marks—triangles, dia-monds, globes or cylinders.

Creeks and small landward channels useable only by boats and barges are rarely buoyed ; but in most cases the edges of the surrounding mud banks are marked by branches cut from trees and planted firmly in the mud.   According to local custom these are known as " perches " " brooms ", or " withies."   Occasionally one comes upon a " spar

buoy " in some narrow channel used by coasting
vessels. This consists of a wooden pole floating on
the surface, and chained by its butt end to a sinker
in the middle of the channel. A spar buoy is used
in these cases because, unlike an iron buoy, there is
no chance of it being damaged if a vessel collides
with it.

Fig. 35.   A marshy creek, with Spar Buoy and "Perches."

Need it be said that a dinghy sailor must be
extremely careful not to let the current sweep his
fragile craft into collision with any buoy or beacon ?
She would be severely harmed, if not capsized, by
the impact.

Earlier in this book the procedure in handling a
boat under sail has been illustrated by imaginary
examples of an hour or two's outing on a tidal
river. The same method will be employed here
with regard to cruising, as it is the one most calcu-
lated to impress the memory, and to impart realism ;
whereas a series of precepts would be boring and
readily forgotten.

As a jumping-off place or, shall we say for grandeur, " port of departure," it will be well to choose the " head of navigation " of some small creek or river to which our 14 ft. centreboard dinghy has been conveyed in advance by road or rail. Places such as this are preferable to commercial ports, because they are quiet. One can launch and provision the boat without collecting a crowd, and the local inn and village shops are usually able, between them, to supply anything in the nature of consumable stores which, by that not uncommon oversight, has been omitted.

If it is possible for you and your crew of one to arrive at the waterfront a good three hours before high water, make a point of doing so ; because you will be glad of the ebb stream to carry you seaward, and it always takes one a matter of hours to launch a boat and stow her gear and commisariat satis-factorily. Should this matter of time and tide have to be left out of consideration for some extraneous reason, it is quite likely that when you turn up there will be nothing but exposed mud. Also on these occasions it has been known to rain !

Under such circumstances there is naturally a temptation to call it a day, and retire to the village inn. But it is much better, unless you have weeks of leisure before you, to get on with the job of preparing for sea, or you may not only miss the tide but a burst of sunshine and a favouring breeze. In boat cruising the opportunity missed is invariably regretted.

The load of sailing gear, kit bags and provision
boxes, though it may appear bulky rather than
heavy, will make the boat far harder to shift about
when aground than before she is laden.   For that
reason if, owing to mud, you cannot actually slide
the boat into the water, drag her down as nearly
as you can to it before loading her.

This business of loading the boat will become a
matter of straightforward routine in a day or two ;
but at first one must scheme it out carefully.   For
a start stow heavy, rectangular objects, such as the
oilstove case and provision tins, on either side of
the centreboard case, wedging them securely with
the kitbags, one of the latter in the round of each
bilge.   The fresh water can or jar should be aft of
the centreboard case, so that you can readily obtain
a drink of water at any time.   Pots and pans, and
any spare gear that will stand bilge water may be
placed between the centreboard case and the mast.
These will serve as " dunnage," a lower layer to
raise the blankets, wrapped in canvas, above—we
hope—the bilge water level.

By the time everything is stowed aboard not much
floor-space will be left for the crew ; but at all costs
the bottom boards must be left clear centrally
between the middle thwart and the stern-seat, since
there, one must have clear foot space both when
sailing and when rowing ; also, as mentioned
previously, there is the bailing well to be kept clear.

When satisfied that all is shipshape, it is time
enough to be considering the inner man who, after

all this exertion, will surely call for his due. A substantial meal now may save attempting an elaborate supper on this first evening, when there may be difficulties, the crew not having as yet shaken down.

This, of course, does not imply that one can afford to linger after high water. It is best to be off and away even before the adverse flood tide is spent ; for in many tidal rivers the ebb stream goes out with a four hours' rush followed by two hours of slack tide, when the current will contribute little to one's progress.

Not only are the above considerations conducive to a prompt start. There may be others in the shape of uncongenial surroundings which you may wish to leave well behind before making camp. Many a tidal stream, starting pleasantly enough, passes through some industrial district as it becomes navigable by coasters, and such reaches as these are nothing better than municipal back-yards.

The faster to get away from these gas works and refuse-tip regions you may be tempted to accept some kindly offer of a tow. Well, be careful. The motor or steam barge that here picks her way at a safe and comfortable four knots may work up to eight knots where the channel widens. For your loaded dinghy the latter speed would be a tremendous strain, and—what is more—she might yaw so wildly as to capsize.

Unless absolutely assured of your towing line being cast off by the steamer on your signal, either forego towing altogether, or else pass your line once only round a bollard or stanchion on the steamer's stern, so that you use the line double, with both ends in your own boat. The ends must both be made fast right against the stem of your boat, the upper end being fast with a "slippery hitch" or half-bow, so that with one jerk on the very end of the rope it will be freed to run out. This arrangement is a "slip line." See to it that, when called upon, it is really going to slip without catching on anything.

If instead of rowing or being towed through an industrialised stretch of river you are under sail, keep watch for violent gusts striking the water between tall buildings. They may be as strong as those emerging from cliff gullies, and must be met with an eased mainsheet. Your boat, being loaded, will not list so sharply to a hard puff as she did when light ; but neither will you be able to luff so smartly to spill the wind. In consequence, relieving the sail of excessive wind pressure must be done by easing out the sheet.

Creeks and rivers broaden towards their mouths. Everyone knows that. But only those who use such waterways are equally aware that the main channel does not widen in the same proportion ; but in many cases is almost as narrow where it threads the estuary as it is higher upstream where it extends from bank to bank. Not only that. It may follow a serpentine course from one shore to the other and, of course, the deep draught traffic has to follow all its convolutions. To be safe from steamers you have to keep clear of the channel, and to that end, before starting out, a chart of the particular estuary should be studied, and the general lie of the channel memorised or reproduced in simple outline in a pocket book. Whether you trust to memory or prepare a sketch this will be better than taking along a bulky, expensive chart and getting it reduced to a pulp, as would inevitably happen.

Even in the case of creeks too shallow for steam traffic one is glad of guidance, for there may be other creeks branching out of them, making it only too easy to lose one's way. Most of these lesser creeks are described and illustrated by " chartlets " in books on yacht pilotage, and such a book is worth taking with you in a waterproof cover.

The chief and inevitable weakness of all charts and " yachtsmen's guides " is that almost as soon as they are published they fall out of date. The channel buoys referred to in the text or chart are far from permanent. They may sink or be washed away and not be replaced. Extra buoys may be laid, beacons be removed or added, and shore marks, such as " conspicuous trees " are all too likely to be cut down.

This may sound very discouraging ; but there are surer guides than books, charts and sea marks in the water itself. Waves in deep water flow straight down wind. On the edge of banks they swing round towards the shallows. at the same time forming steep ridges that break into foam with regularity. There are other signs, too, such as

B

eddies and changes of colour, which will all tell you something about the seabed once you have acquired " sea sense " by practising pilotage.

Owing to the slowness of any small and heavily laden boat it will be found necessary to make as much use as possible of favourable currents, and to avoid adverse ones. A tidal current will often be met with that runs faster than the boat can sail, and so its direction makes all the difference.

On this first day's run down-river towards the sea, you may have the benefit of fresh water from up-river reinforcing the ebb tide, and so be pushed along for six hours by a favourable current. That, however, is by no means always the case. The ebb may only run for four hours, and the succeeding flood tide may come in with such a rush that for the next five or six hours further progress is impossible.

Sitting in an anchored boat for a matter of five hours waiting for the tide to turn, is an occupation that palls at the best of times, and by now evening probably is approaching and it is time to pitch camp. If such a tidal hold-up has found you in a spot where the channel is hundreds of yards from the shore, it will be worth your while either to plug on, however slowly, against the tide or else run back, to some point where the foreshore is steeper and shorter.

There run the boat in, and carry the anchor as far up the bank as possible, and stamp it into the ground. This must always be done before unloading the boat, or someday the rising tide will play a trick on you, carrying the boat off with it. A long swim might well be involved in recovering her.

How to snug down for the night, choosing the best spot and rigging shelter to the best advantage, is only learnt by experience. Beginners are apt to spread their bedding on hard, uncomfortable ground, sometimes too low, where they are invaded by the tide, sometimes too high, where chilly night winds insinuate draughts into the " bivvy," and make sleep impossible.

On a really nasty night of wind and rain it is best to sleep in the boat, however cramped the space ; because at least you will be dry underneath, and it will not involve exposing the kit while a tent or shelter is erected.

On this first evening, assuming you have beginner's luck with the weather, a quick search should be made of the local terrain for either small well-rounded shingle or wiry herbage at a safe height above high-water mark. Either of these will make a much more comfortable bed than field grass or sand, and you want to be quite three feet above the highest tide mark ; because a low barometer and a strong wind out at sea might possibly send in an exceptionally high night tide and—literally— catch you napping.

A site having been chosen, a satisfactory shelter can be rigged up in the following way.

Bring the mast and oars ashore, and lash the latter together at the neck of their handles. Step their blade tips into the ground, and form a tripod with the oars and mast, securing the head of the latter in the crutch formed by the crossed oar handles. Arrange this tripod with the foot of the mast towards the wind, and drape the sail over it, so that the only opening left is between the oars. Then bring in the kit and bedding, and drag the dinghy close to windward as a windbreak. With sand or shingle heaped round the edges of the sail to steady it and exclude draughts, you will find this makeshift tent surprisingly comfortable.

CHAPTER XII

THE OPEN COAST

If the reader has inferred that boat cruising about a shallow estuary is a mild sort of adventuring, with but minor risks for any sensible, wide-awake individual, he will have guessed rightly. The worst that is at all likely to happen is a capsize in shallow surf, resulting in a soaked kit and spoilt food.

Coastwise cruising in an open boat calls for more experience and even greater vigilance, for the sea is not an element with which one can take liberties. Let us suppose that, after a few days pottering about our shallow estuary, it is decided to take advantage of the promise of calm, sunny weather and extend the trip beyond the estuary's confines. If the boat has not to be sailed back to her starting point, it is advisable—other things being equal—to follow the coast in the more down-wind direction, so as to reel off the miles with greater certainty. But if she must be brought back and time presses, obviously it is better to beat up against the prevailing direction of the wind, so that there will be the likelihood of a quick return passage.

In any case, a decision on this point should be made before the mouth of the estuary is approached ; because in almost all cases the shoals fan outwards towards the sea, with the channels like spread fingers between them. Crossing the mouth of an estuary involves crossing shoals and channels alternately, and sailing beam-on to the tidal current as well. Such a passage may lead through very choppy water, and sailing across strong tidal currents may result in the boat being swept a long way sideways, either back towards the river, or right out to sea, where you might completely lose your bearings.

Much of the fascination of such a journey as this, down a river and through an estuary to the sea, lies in the steadily increasing evidences of the latter's influence as you approach nearer and nearer to open water, till at last the sea becomes paramount, with its clear, green surges pounding the pebbles, and its tides running free among rocks ; whereas at the start of your trip it crept turbidly among the sedges. This gives one a sense of travelling—something quite distinct from going down to the sea by rail.

After reminding the reader yet once again that the sea stands no nonsense from careless and inexpert folk in open boats, it remains to add a few hints about landing on an open beach, should the sea in its perversity force you to come ashore in a hurry without selecting some inlet or rock-screened cove where a landing would be easier.

Viewed from seaward, waves breaking on a beach appear round-backed and easy to steer through, because their crests are on their forward faces. The same waves would disclose their formidable character only if you saw them from the shore. For this reason be more careful than appears necessary. While still in deep water lower the sail and unstep the mast. Roll them together, and stow them in such a way that they cannot impede your rowing. If the mast must project, let it do so over the bows, leaving the stern unencumbered.

Next, roll up your trousers for wading, as you are bound to jump overboard to haul the boat up, and then clear the anchor and its rope, except for the " bitter end " (the end not on the anchor), which should be made fast forward. Naturally, as you approach the breakers slowly under oars, it becomes somewhat easier to take stock of them, and one can decide whether it is possible, by making a spurt, to drive straight in to the beach on a big wave, as one would on a surf board ; or whether there are too many rows of small steep waves, and too much backwash for this to be feasible.

In the latter case one must back in, stern foremost, checking the boat as each wave strikes the bows and rowing hard astern in the troughs only. If the anchor rope is long—say 100 feet—drop the anchor overside when you are about that distance from the beach, and as the rope pays out over the bows check it each time the boat lifts to a comber. This will keep her end-on. To be driven broadside-on is to be rolled over.

Before the boat grounds on her final shoreward rush, jump overboard, one on each side, and pull her in. This must be done without a second's hesitation, or the backwash may sweep her down the beach sideways into the next wave.

Never, even if single-handed, pull the boat in from a position behind the transom, but only from the quarter ; because, should a wave fling the boat up the beach, there would almost certainly be an accident if you stood in her path—a crushed foot or maybe some worse injury.

Launching a boat through surf, though often a wet and strenuous undertaking, is less fraught with risk of a capsize than beaching her, for you can see what you are up against, and can wait for a large wave to break, and then carry you out on its backwash. Wade out with the boat as deeply as possible, and on jumping aboard pole out with the oars into deeper water. There is no time for shipping the oars in the rowlocks. The boat must be kept forging ahead, or she will be swept sideways and capsized in the backwash. The secret of success lies in selecting just the right moment to float the boat, and then acting without hesitation.

Whether one is beaching or launching a boat it is a wave larger than the others that one must utilize. The reader has no doubt heard of the " third wave," popularly supposed to be larger than two before and two after it ; but the notably big ones arrive at much longer intervals. On our western coasts, where they are open to the Atlantic, ten or twelve minutes may elapse between the incidence of large waves, and the longer the interval the bigger they are. Even two days after a gale very large solitary swells of the " mountain high " variety are likely on exposed coasts, and for these a wary eye must be kept on the seaward horizon ; because they suddenly steepen and break at distances from the shore where smaller swells pass harmlessly.

One other type of sea disturbance must be dealt with here, because such risks as boat cruising presents are almost entirely the outcome of surprise and ignorance—the sea is so like a fierce-looking dog, which only attacks those who are uncomprehending and show timidity towards it !

The class of disturbances in question are " races " or " tide rips " and " overfalls," which are rapids caused by the tide coursing over an uneven area of seabed.

Races are common round our coasts, the worst ones being off rocky headlands or in narrow channels between islands. Overfalls are caused by submerged rock ledges or steep, narrow shoals of sand or shingle, forming natural weirs. The main disturbance is on their down-stream side.

In either case there is a period of half-an-hour or so at high and low tide, when the waves drop and a boat can pass ; but otherwise you must keep right away. The roar of the tossing, foaming water can be heard for miles, so there is small chance of driving towards a race unawares. Most tidal races can be avoided by stealing past them on the in-shore side, almost touching the beach, where there will often be a fairly calm belt of water a few yards

wide, unless the wind happens to be strong and
blowing the waves towards the shore.

Unlike larger craft, small boats are but little
endangered by fog, because they can be stopped or
turned within a few feet of an obstruction, and the
swell breaking on a shoal is heard in ample time
for you to change course and avoid it. In a fog
most ships move slowly; so there is usually but
little danger of your being run down. On the
other hand, the ferry steamers between this country
and France and Belgium travel at speed even in
the thickest weather, so in the Straits of Dover one
must proceed past harbour mouths with caution.

In spite of it being reasonably safe to continue
along the coast in a fog, few will want to do so
unless pressed for time, and to reach the shore at
the nearest point though blinded by the smother one
should act in the following way : When you see the
fog coming, head the boat for the shore, and note
which point of your compass is in line with the boat'
keel. Lay the compass in the bottom of the boat, and
watching it to see it points the same way the whole
time, row steadily shoreward till the boat grounds
This calls for no knowledge of the compass's naviga
tional use nor of its various errors. You steer so
that its card or needle remains pointing the same
way steadily, and that is all.

CHAPTER XIII

RACING

SINCE to at least half the owners of sailing boats racing is the prime interest, it may appear scant justice to this branch of our sport to consign it to one short chapter. The reason for this is the opposite of what may be supposed. It is because racing is a subject too comprehensive to be properly dealt with here. The reader if " bitten " with racing should study books that are more advanced and at the same time concerned in the main with racing craft, not general purpose and cruising dinghies.

As far as the actual handling of the tiller and sheets during a race is concerned the man who has cruised in open sailing boats will find that he has not a great deal to learn. In a hard breeze on an open water course he may, in fact, do better than many of those who have had no cruising experience. Steering and sheet trimming is, however, only a part of the racing game. Of the fifty Racing Rules laid down by the Royal Yachting Association, no less than fifteen are directed to the governance of the master of a vessel in the course of a race; and securing a win depends in no small measure on the correct interpretation of them. While taking every

permissable advantage of his opponents the experienced racing skipper is careful not to overstep the
restrictions either in the spirit or the letter.

The very simple International Rule of the Road
at Sea may well appear to the novice as quite
sufficient to prevent collisions occurring in the course
of a race. This code lays it down that a sailing
craft close-hauled on the port tack shall give way
to one close-hauled on the starboard tack ; that
a boat sailing free shall give way to both of them ;
and that no craft shall crowd another into a position
of danger. Unquestionably these simple rules
would suffice were racing under sail merely a
straight-forward speed contest ; but that is not the
case. Long before there were yacht and sailing
clubs as we know them, yachts were associated in
" squadrons," like the Royal Yacht Squadron, and
in " fleets " such as the Cumberland Fleet. In
those days yachts were volunteer naval auxiliaries,
and tactical exercises were carried out as a main
feature of the season's programme. The naval
value of smart sail handling, though a thing of the
past, has left an echo, and the racing rules of today
foster an interest in competitive manoeuvre, that
results in a sailing match being something much
more than a simple speed contest. Were this not
realised, it might come as a shock to the observer
to see yachts deliberately " blanketing " their
opponents (masking their sails from the wind), or
steering to cross their bows so that they have to get
out of the way to avoid a collision. In practice

you will find that this manoeuvring and counter-manoeuvring adds tremendously to the spice of boat racing ; but we must now turn to the pre-liminary details—preparing your boat for a race, and coming up to the starting line.

An essential preliminary, that should receive attention well in advance of a race, is an unhurried examination of all the gear, from the centreboard tackle to the halliard sheave at the masthead. Friction and corrosion both make constant small renewals necessary, and one must bear in mind the fact that every cord, cleat and block may be tested to the limit of its strength in the course of the coming race. New cordage, on the other hand, always wants stretching and breaking-in ; so a practice spin before the race is necessary to ensure that the new stuff will not give trouble by becoming slack or by twisting into kinks and tangles.

Unless the club or regatta committee's rules forbid it, the boat should, if possible, be out of the water for a day or two before racing, in order to dry her planking and so reduce her weight. This may sound a trivial matter ; but for racing in light airs it is most important. Polishing a boat's bottom may possibly be disallowed ; but this also has a notably beneficial effect on her speed.

From the club's officer of the day, or whoever else is in charge of the racing arrangements, one must obtain precise details as to the starting time and the course to be sailed, with special reference as to which turning marks, such as buoys and anchored boats are to be " left to port " or " left to starboard." Should you pass on the wrong side of any mark, or touch it with your craft in passing during the race, you will be disqualified.

Small boat courses practically always have the same line for the finish as for the start. This imaginary line will extend from the shore below the club's signal mast, or a mast or staff on a committee boat, to a post, buoy or anchored boat opposite, across the water.

Those organizing minor racing events cannot always be relied on to start the boats off in the manner prescribed by the R.Y.A., and enquiries should be tactfully made as to the local procedure.

The orthodox method of regulating the start of a race is as follows : Ten minutes before the actual start of the race an International Code flag, generally the white and blue swallowtail " A," is hoisted on the signal mast. Your boat should be ready to get under way and, if you have one, your private oblong racing flag, of distinctive design should be on its swivel pin above the mast truck.

Five minutes after the first signal the " A " flag is replaced by the " Blue Peter," a blue bordered oblong flag with a white oblong centre, and as the latter reaches the masthead the " first gun " is fired. From the firing of this gun to the end of the race competing craft are bound by the racing rules and cannot infringe them without being disqualified.

Five minutes after the first gun the actual start of the race will be signalled by firing the gun again and lowering the Blue Peter. Before that, all the competing craft will have set their canvas and manoeuvred into position close to the starting line, so as to be able to cross it immediately after the firing of the starting gun. If the wind blows across the course one should aim for the windward end of the line, so as not to be blanketed by opponents. But this coveted position is sought by everyone, with the result that they obstruct each other. As a consequence, it sometimes pays to seek a leeward berth where there is clear space to cross the line at top speed. This is a nice point in tactics.

In his eagerness to waste no time behind the line once the second gun has been fired and the race has started, many a helmsman, in spite of a carefully observed stop-watch, misjudges his speed and distance, and crosses the line too early. If he does so his boat will be re-called, probably by megaphone. But whether he hears this signal or not his boat will be out of the race until he has returned behind the line and made a fresh start. Having to come back like this is practically certain to put the boat at the tail of the fleet for the time being. In a race that lasts several hours this bad start may not prove a great handicap; but a few minutes, or even seconds, lost at the commencement of a short race make a very great difference.

Although the R.Y.A. racing Rules of the Road call for a far more detailed analysis than can be attempted in this small book, a few notes on the system will not be out of place.

To begin with, although the fifty rules appear a

formidable codex in themselves, there is in addition a mass of " footnotes " tacked on to the Rules, also the dicta and awards pronounced by the Council of the R.Y.A. in its role of a court of appeal. This " case law " is constantly being added to and varied, and so, like the Laws of England, the racing rules are only to be interpreted with certainty by those who make a special study of them.

Probably this uncertainty and complication are inevitable ; but they do result in a regrettable number of "protests," and encourage the sea-lawyer element that is to be found in racing circles. One should make it a matter of principle never to protest unless certain of having been obstructed in a manner contrary to the racing rules. If, however, there is that certainty, by all means tie a flag or handkerchief in your rigging ; for this signal has got to be clearly displayed to the race committee the next time you pass their stand.

The racing rule over which you are most likely to be drawn into a protest case is Rule 30, Clause " b " of which is referred to as " the luffing rule." The relevant part of Rule 30 is worded as follows : " Overtaking.—Of two yachts, sailing the same or nearly the same course, one which is clear astern of another when approaching her, so as to involve risk of collision, is said to be an overtaking yacht, and she continues such after the yachts overlap until she has again drawn clear.

(*a*) A yacht overtaking another shall keep out of the way of the overtaken yacht.

(b) Provided that the overtaking yacht makes her overlap on the side opposite to that on which the overtaken yacht then carries her main boom, the latter may luff as she pleases to prevent the former passing her to windward, until she is in such a position that her bowsprit end, or stem if she has no bowsprit, would strike the overtaking yacht abaft the main shrouds."

The general effect of this rule is that if you are sailing towards a mark to windward and an opponent comes up on you from your weather quarter you may edge up as close to the wind as you can without tacking, and force him to do the same to keep out of the way. If he cannot sail as close to the wind as you can he will lose speed and drop behind, which is what you want him to do.

On the face of it, this rule appears to make it quite clear as to which of two yachts or boats engaged in a " luffing match " may legitimately force the other off her course ; but in practice the words " overtaking " and " overlapping " are variously construed in spite of " footnotes " to the rules which purport to crystallize the matter. This uncertainty, it need hardly be said, gives our sea-lawyers many an opportunity for what they most enjoy—an interminable wrangle.

Since the reader's first boat will not, if he is well advised, be of the racing type, but rather a sturdy knockabout, he will have no chance of winning races from scratch against out-and-out racing craft even of obsolete type. However, plenty of handicap events are organised by sailing clubs, in which every boat has a chance, and we may conclude with a few words on " time allowances."

For levelling up the chances of yachts of varied sizes and types there are measurement rules that work satisfactorily, giving the slower craft so many extra seconds per mile in which to complete the course ; but the small boats that turn out for club and village events are usually such a mixed bag that they can only be handicapped in the light of their past and expected performances.

Whatever handicap is allotted you makes no difference at the start of the race—all the boats start together—but their finishing times are all noted down and " corrected " by deducting each boat's time allowance of so many minutes and seconds. On corrected time the last boat to cross the finishing line may quite possibly win the race if she has been given the longest time allowance.

CHAPTER XIV

EMERGENCIES AND EXPEDIENTS

HERE and there in the preceding chapters the hint has been dropped that not every sailing manoeuvre necessarily proceeds according to plan, emergencies arising that call for special measures.

Such emergencies are of two distinct kinds : those personal to the boat sailor, involving his own craft directly, and the other sort, where his assistance is needed to get someone else out of trouble.

The personal emergency calls for our first attention, because only when one has learnt how to get out of a " jam " is one competent to assist others who may be ignorant of the right procedure.

Tidal creeks and natural harbours are the favourite sailing grounds for small boats ; but almost all of such waters abound in mud banks on which even the most wary occasionally get stranded. " Hitting the putty " causes one no great inconvenience if the tide is rising, for automatically it will float one free as long as the boat is not allowed to drive further into the bank. On the other hand, if the tide is ebbing one may be stranded in inglorious isolation for any time up to ten hours.

To get off a mud bank when the tide is falling,

speed is essential. Drop the sail, lift the centre-board and unship the rudder. Then row hard to bring the boat off stern-first. If the first dozen strokes show no result, do not continue rowing. That would be useless, because the boat is all the time settling into the mud. Instead, get your shoes off and trousers rolled high, and step overboard, holding on to the boat. With the mud very soft this, of course, is unpleasant ; but it will make the boat draw less water so that rocking and pushing her astern is almost certain to get her afloat. It need scarcely be added that one must keep hold of the gunwale the whole time while overboard ; otherwise one is likely to make a much closer acquaintance with the mud.

Of this latter substance or, to be more accurate, semi-fluid, many people are terrified, and in their fear lies its real danger. A man who finds that his legs are sinking further and further into mud or quicksand instinctively struggles to maintain his upright balance, and this it is that drives him in. If you cannot free your legs, and there is no one to haul you out, lean right back till your shoulders touch the mud, with arms outspread, and you will sink no further. The legs can then be cautiously wriggled free, and by using your feet and hands as in swimming while in the prone position, you will win to firm ground or to the water. In the latter case swim on your back till there is a sufficient depth of water for the breast or side stroke.

Next to running aground, the beginner's most

likely mishap is a capsize, usually the direct result of some error of judgment.

The most common of such mistakes is under-estimating the wind's strength in the offing when setting out from the shore. One may also be lulled into a sense of false security by a light and steady breeze, and so be taken unawares when a violent gust, emerging from under some hard edged cloud or from a gap in a line of cliffs, lays the boat flat in an instant.

Neither luffing into the wind nor easing away the sheet will sufficiently relieve the sail of wind pressure if the whole mainsail happens to be set when a really strong squall strikes an open sailing boat. Unless you manage to get the sail down with a run immediately—and that is far from easy—she will turn over.

Another frequent cause of small sailing boats upsetting is the loss of balance caused by the helmsman or his crew getting tangled in some part of the running gear, such as the fall of the mainsheet, at the very moment when a strong gust, striking the sail, needs counteracting by the crew, as " live ballast," leaning out over the weather gunwale. This comes of carelessness, the coiled lines not having been tucked away safely.

An initial mishap, which may quickly lead to a capsize may be such an apparent trifle as the jamming or slipping of a rope. As an instance, the sheave carrying the main halliard at the masthead may be a loose fit in the slot in the mast, allowing the halliard to slip sideways off the sheave, and become firmly jammed in the slot, so that the sail cannot be lowered. This would be a serious matter in face of a violent squall.

To clear the jam, first try pushing the blade of an oar up between the halliard and the mast to lift the halliard back on to its sheave. If this fails, row the boat round head to wind, collect the sail and boom into a bundle, which can be tied to the mast, and then unstep the latter, so that you can reach the masthead. Needless to say, in a lumpy sea this must be done very carefully.

No harm is likely to come of a halliard slipping off its cleat or belaying pin ; but if the tack rope should come loose any lugsail will fly up into the air, and by its furious gyrations make the boat almost impossible to balance. As in the last case, row the boat head to wind—a single oar used on the leeward side will do it —and you can then grab hold of the sail and lower it. In such cases as the above, where one is forced to stand up in a tossing boat, the most important factor is a firm foothold, and bare feet are best.

Finally it should be noted that a boat, jostled by confused waves, can capsize to windward. This mishap is brought about by the crew sitting up on the weather gunwale and " hiking " (leaning right out as far as possible) to balance a large spread of sail in a strong wind. Should the wind suddenly lighten the crew has got to dart back just as quickly into the boat. If he is too slow, his weight will turn her over against the wind.

In this one instance the crew will be " thrown into the water " as they say in the papers. The ordinary capsize to leeward is a much slower affair. For what seems an age the water hovers about your lee gunwale, curls, and finally comes down in a cascade. Then at last the boat begins to right herself ; but, of course, it is too late, and she goes on filling till both gunwales are dipping under water. However, there is little fear of a centreboard boat sinking unless metal or stone has been put on board as ballast, a professional waterman's custom that should on no account be followed.

Provided that one is within easy swimming distance of the shore, or help is at hand, there is little danger entailed in the swamping of a boat that cannot sink. If your boat should have a heavy iron centreboard she should also have sealed oil drums or petrol cans fixed under the thwarts to make up the lost buoyancy. About six gallons total capacity is likely to prove sufficient ; but a test should be made by swamping the boat in shallow water.

To be involved in a capsize far from the shore, or amongst breakers and rocks is a very serious matter because of one's helplessness once the boat has filled. It is impossible to bail out a swamped boat except in a stark calm or after she has been beached. All one can do is to bundle the gear under the thwarts, so that it does not float away, and support oneself by holding on to the gunwale. Under such conditions the temptation to leave the swamped boat and try to swim to the shore is very strong ; but usually it is further off than it looks, and leaving the boat may prove the worse choice of two evils. It may be that though the accident was observed the collecting of a crew and the launching of a suitable boat are taking time, a quarter of an hour perhaps, which seems an age when one is waiting for help, and possibly drifting seaward. If you should decide to swim for the shore, kick off your shoes and trousers before abandoning the boat.

Except as the sequel to capsizing, a small open sailing boat is unlikely to be blown right away from the land ; because even if the mast should break one is almost certain to have a pair of oars on board, with which to row back. However, novices sometimes do the most incredibly foolish things, and sailing a dinghy offshore without oars aboard is one of them.

If with this lack of prevision the mast should break or the rudder in any way be put out of action, usually there is only one possible expedient : Pull up the burthen boards and wrench one loose. Then, after lowering the mast, sit right in the bows, and with the board paddle the boat stern-foremost. Try and keep the wind on the starboard quarter while paddling over the port bow—now to your right—and you will make fair progress unless the wind is really strong.

The ability to scull with a single oar from a notch in the transom is an accomplishment the boat sailor should acquire at an early stage of his novitiate. It may come in handily if an oar is lost overboard.

Stand facing aft. Grip the oar handle with both hands, knuckles up, and trail the oar blade flat on the water. Then with a clockwise wrist movement dip the blade towards your right, and push the handle to your left, and on completing the stroke exactly reverse this process. At each stroke the blade will be driven under by its inclination ; but one's trouble at first is to keep the loom of the oar in the transom notch. This will be easiest if you scull against a very light headwind, which will tend to push the boat backwards against the thrust of the oar. The latter must be straight, not spoon, bladed.

Perhaps it is some consolation, when one considers the grim fact that a small boat can be driven right away from the land by the wind, that she is most unlikely to be swamped so long as the occupants have sufficient presence of mind to throw any heavy articles overboard, and then sit in the bottom. A boat that yields to the waves and is buoyant can survive in a very nasty sea, a fact which accounts for the ocean voyages that have been made in ships' lifeboats.

The " Chivalry of the Sea " is not merely a fine phrase, it is a reality ; and it is up to all of us who use salt water to uphold it. Never be shy of offering help, because inexpert assistance is better than none, and the other fellow may be sufficiently experienced to direct your efforts.

Should someone else's boat run on the mud, you can be of the greatest assistance by first taking off the crew to lighten her instead of their having to get overboard for that purpose. To reach the stranded boat lower all sail, and row in stern first till the transoms meet. With your painter as a tow rope you can then pull the other boat off stern foremost.

The great majority of boating mishaps, where one may usefully lend a hand, are of the type described, where there is no serious danger. On the other hand, the day may come when as the nearest or only person in the vicinity with a boat, one is called upon to save a life.

In most of such cases it is not so much headlong courage as cool resource that is required. The former may merely make matters worse, with two people floundering helplessly in the water instead of one. Any rescue at sea has to be planned with full regard to all the circumstances—wind strength, tidal currents, depth of water, character of the waves, and your boat's manoeuvreability.

As already pointed out, the commonest direct cause of a capsize is a violent gust of wind ; but it can also result from over-loading, bad watermanship or the unseaworthiness of the boat herself.

On observing that a boat has upset one must gauge the urgency of the case ; because one would prefer to approach under oars, and so make certain of grasping a swimmer at the first attempt. But if it appears that there is a man drowning already, and you can make better speed under sail, carry on and take the hit-or-miss chance. With the sail and tiller to control, you will not find it easy in rough water ; but bear in mind just how you luff up into the wind when picking up a mooring buoy, and proceed in the same manner, bringing the swimmer abreast the weather bow just as your boat loses way. On no account attempt to pick the man up when sailing fast with the wind over the stern, it would be hopeless. You must get to leeward of him first, and then, as we have said, luff up to him. Matters are somewhat eased by the fact that both the swimmer and your boat are equally affected by any current running at the time. It cannot carry you past him in the way it might carry you past an anchored object.

To give a clearer and more detailed picture of the *modus operandi* of a rescue, we may take the likely case of the reader some day being alone in a small sailing dinghy on the open sea on a breezy day, and his seeing a similar craft with one man aboard capsize some few hundred yards to leeward.

Since you are to windward and the breeze is fresh, you naturally will make the approach under sail. If the other man is holding on to his boat, and clearly in no immediate danger, it will be best to sail down to leeward, lower the canvas, and come up to him under oars. In that way you will not risk a collision with the swamped boat, which might capsize your own. Coming right close, you will enable him to grasp your boat's gunwale. Help him to work round to the transom, unship the rudder out of his way, and then yourself move to the bows to balance the boat while he climbs aboard over the stern.

In the other case, where the crew has been washed

away from his swamped boat, and has gone under once, or shown other signs of helplessness, you will have to gybe or round in your mainsheet as you run past him, and then, sailing close-hauled till within a few feet of him, push down the tiller, so as to spill the wind from the sail, and come to a halt with the man against your weather bow. At that you must jump forward and grab him. There will be no time to lower the sail ; though the latter flogging about, may upset your boat if left standing many seconds untended.

For that reason pass your boat's painter round the man in the water below his arms as quickly as ever you can Pull the rope tight, and secure its free end to the middle thwart. This will keep his head above water while you lower the sail and unship the rudder

As in the other case, you have next to get your man round to the transom ; but we are assuming that he is helpless, so you will have to free him from the painter, pull his hands over the gunwale, and carefully edge him to the stern.

It is at this point that you are likely to find yourself " up against it " ; because the half-drowned man will be helpless and need to be pulled on board ; and when you go to the stern and try to lift him, his weight and yours combined will most likely pull the top of the transom under water. You may just manage to get him on board, if strong enough, to land him with one quick heave. That, however, is not to be anticipated, owing to the wild motion of your boat and the extra weight of sodden clothing.   On

finding you cannot lift the man, get the mainsheet or
some other line round him and secure him with his
head and shoulders above the transom edge. In
that position he is safe while you row him ashore.
Such treatment sounds rough, but it is the best you
can manage. As soon as you are in water shallow
enough for wading, get overboard, unlash the man,
and carry him to the beach ; for he might be in-
jured if still dragging from the stern as your boat
grounded.

It need hardly be added that with a larger boat,
say 15 ft. long, or with two of a crew, matters are
much easier than in a case such as the above ; for
in either instance your boat can be steadied on a
fairly even keel, allowing the person in the water to
be lifted aboard over the transom without great
difficulty.

In coastal boating the problem of rescuing a
person stranded on a rock is almost as likely a one as
that of picking up the crew of a swamped boat.
Bathers and venturesome boys scrambling about the
boulders of a steep-to shore are liable to be caught by
the tide and ringed about with surf that may sweep
them into the dangerous backwash.

In this case, if the surf is at all heavy, one dare not
let the boat touch the rock, or she and you will be
rolled over together. Should you have an anchor,
and ropes which can be joined to form a temporary
anchor cable fifty or more feet long, drop the anchor
just clear of the breakers, and " veer " down to the
rock by paying out the rope from the bows, as life-

boatmen do when approaching a stranded vessel.
You can then play your boat, allowing her to run in
on a wave crest, to let the stranded person jump for
the stern, and again pull out clear of the rock before
the wave subsides. Without a rope and anchor you
would have to back in under oars, and pull out the
same way ; but that method is much more dangerous
on account of the difficulty of rowing in broken
water.

In any of the emergencies with which we have
dealt it may prove necessary to jettison the sailing
gear of one's boat together with any personal kit
that is aboard, so as to lighten the craft and clear her
for action.

It is the way of Davy Jones to demand these small
offerings of those that rob him of a human sacrifice.

Anchor 131, 146, 151, 173.

Backstay, 94.
Backwash, 151, 152, 173.
Bailer, 129, 130.
Balance Lug, 99, 101.
Batten, 97, 102, 104.
Beacon, 139.
Belaying Pin, 16.
Bermudian sail, 52, 65, 91, 93,
    96, 97, 101, 102, 116.
Block, 18, 19.
Blue Peter, 158.
Boom, 15, 17, 26, 36, 38, 39, 40,
    42, 59, 68, 69, 87 (36-42).
Bridle, 76.
Bumkin, 73, 79, 80.

Canoe, 102.
Capsize, 22.
Centreboard, 12, 23, 38, 41, 46,
    50, 61-3, 80, 81, 109, 123.
Chinese Lug, 99, 101, 102.
Clamp, 12.
Cleat, 16, 41, 69, 77, 85.
Clew, 21, 43.
Club, 107.
Coir Rope, 131.
Compass, 131, 154.
Cringle, 40, 42, 44, 73.
Cruising Ground, 137.

Dagger Plate, 12.
Dinghy, 9, 47.
Dipping Lug, 99, 100.
Dunnage, 142.

Eyebolt, 17.

Fairlead, 74.
Flax Cord, 119.
Fog, 131, 154.

Foresail, 56.
Forestay, 80.

Gaff, 67, 98.
Goose-neck, 68, 69, 97.
Grannie, 43, 44.
Grapnel, 77.
Gudgeon, 13.
Gunter Lug, 65, 67, 79.

Halliard, 15, 17, 23, 25, 41, 66,
    70.
Handicap, 162.
Hanks, 72, 80.
Headboard, 97.
Hiking, 115, 166.
Hog, 19.
Horse, 19, 25, 80.
Hove-to, 86.

Jaws, 66-8, 96.
Jib, 54, 64, 70, 73, 79, 82.
Jibe, 36, 46.

Keel, 23.
Kit Bag, 142.
Knee, 111.

Lace, 21, 22, 82, 98.
Leeboard, 115.
Lift, 104.
Live Ballast, 165.
Luffing Match, 161.
Lugsail, 13, 17, 40, 49, 54, 64,
    65.

Mast, 11, 15, 23, 53, 91, 92, 96.
Mooring, 75 (75-8), 76, 77, 78,
    83, 84, 88 (88-90), 89, 90.
Moulded Construction, 111, 112.

Norfolk Broads, 137.

175

Oars, 23, 27, 34, 41, 46, 87, 130, 168.
Oil Drum, 167.
One-design, 107.
Outboard Motor, 130.
Overfall, 153.

Painter, 24, 27, 47, 170.
Parrel, 104.
Peak, 21.
Pendant, 42, 43, 69.
Pinching, 31, 62.
Primus Stove, 133.
Purchase, 18, 19.

Racing Rules, 155, 156, 159 (159-61), 160, 161.
Reef, 30, 40-2.
Reef Knot, 43-5.
Roller Gear, 69, 72, 83, 116.
Rowlock, 23, 27, 87, 130.
Rudder, 13, 23.
Runner, 94.
Sail Coat, 118.
Sharpie, 113.
Sheet, 19, 25.
Shroud, 92.
Slides, 94.

Slippery Hitch, 25, 144.
Sougimougi, 122.
Spinnaker, 59, 61.
Spreader, 92.
Spritsail, 98.
Step, 12.
Stern Line, 24, 25, 27.
Strop, 15.

Tackle, 80, 81.
Tail, 97.
Tent, 133.
Thwart, 11, 12, 16, 23.
Thumb Cleat, 16.
Tiller, 13, 23, 26, 27.
Tingle, 108, 125.
Towing, 143.
Transom, 10, 19, 170, 172.
Traveller, 15.
Trot, 76.

Varnish, 121.

Wax, 119.

Yard, 15, 16, 25, 41, 67.
Yaw, 35, 39.

Zigzag, 35.